LOVE

THE

Unfinished CHAPTER

DR. LARON MATTHEWS

Published in the United States of America by: LJM Publishing
Publishing Consultant & Interior design by ChosenButterfly Publishing
www.cb-publishing.com
Editing by Stephanie Montgomery, Unique Communications Concepts
Cover design by: World Exhibit Marketing by Jermone Durante

ISBN: 978-1-945377-03-7
First Edition Printing
Printed in the United States of America
October 2017

Table of Contents......

Introduction

Love is a universal word and many people have lived their lives in pursuit of it. A common tapestry that connects us together is our need to be loved, yet many people mistake lust for love. As a result of this, they end up with deep scars and pain in the soul, and an inability to receive and give love. The walls of protection now encase the heart as a protective shield not allowing love to enter in.

This book chronicles my life experiences, drawing lessons from the things that transpired in my life. It has become a tool for teaching others how to avoid similar pitfalls. Moreover, it clearly demonstrates who the oracle of love is, and how to gain entrance to His shrine. In addition, it shows its readers the right path to obtain "true love" and what the three most powerful words in the universe "I love you" really means. If you are longing to experience true love this book is for you! If you are trying to understand why your life has been a cycle of failed relationships this book is for you! Watch your love life develop into what it was meant to be from the beginning.

Dr. Laron Matthews

Foreword. . . . . . .

Prophet Laron Matthews has done an excellent job in the presentation of this book, *Love: The Unfinished Chapter*. This book speaks to me as well as people everywhere who have experienced love, want to experience love, and to those who have experience pain, and scars in their quest for love.

As a Pastor and Bishop, I have seen firsthand the transformative power of the life-giving love of God, as well as the adverse effects of a lack of love in all facets of life. Laron has done a thorough job in the writing of this book, and although, he is talking about agape love, he also gives step by step instructions on how to achieve the finish work of Eros and Philia Love.

Dr. Matthews is accurate in saying to know God is to know love. 1st John 4:7 *Beloved let us love one another for Love is of God and everyone who loveth is born of God and knoweth God.*

I encourage you to read this book it will change your entire life, however it is that you have dealt with love before, you will truly appreciate this book. It will answer the questions that has been on the mind of countless people: Can I experience love again after a divorce? Can God love someone like me? How can I get pass the pain of a broken heart? This is a must read!

God bless you, man of God for allowing the Lord to work in and through your life and to bring you to this place to be a mouthpiece not only to the kingdom of God but to the world at large.

Bishop Rance Allen of the Rance Allen Group
Jurisdictional Prelate of Michigan
Northwestern Harvest
New Bethel Church Of God In Christ
Toledo, Ohio

Endorsements . . . . . .

This is a very aspiring and anointed man of God. I knew Prophet Laron Matthews was special the moment I met him, I could see the love of God in him. Prophet Matthews, spoke to me of things that happen in my life that only God and I knew. When one has been through the hurt and pain of love one can become bitter or better. As you read this book you will see how the power of God's love touched this awesome man's life.

~Martha Hawkins, CEO/Owner of Martha's Place Buffet & Catering; Montgomery, Alabama

Love: The Unfinished Chapter written by Dr. Laron Matthews takes you on a journey that will teach you in many areas of love but most of all how to close those unfinished chapters in your life. This book will bless your life. God bless you Dr. Prophet Laron Matthews! The best is yet to come!

~ Retha Bryant, Administrator Prophet Laron Matthews Ministries

Love is a word that is said by many including those who have no concept of what it really is. This book will help identify the right concepts of love by exposing the erroneous concepts people believe and the damaging consequences of those beliefs. It is my honor and a privilege to be the publishing consultant for this powerful book. Read it and be blessed.

~ Ayanna Moore, CEO/Founder ChosenButterfly Publishing www.cb-publishing.com

Chapter One

When Love Rescued Death at the Door

It began the summer of 1991 at about 3:15 a.m., when I was awakened by a loud knock at my front door. Upon opening the door, I found a close friend with children crying, moaning, and breathing heavily. They appeared very tired and hungry. Something about the children's innocence and the pain in their eyes gripped the deepest part of my soul. There are no words to explain what I saw and experienced.

I could not believe what I was seeing. I had to swallow really hard and take a deep breath because death literally knocked at my door. Pain clutched my heart and for that moment, all I felt was love and compassion. At this very moment, I was coming to terms with a terrible battle evident in the bloodline. *There were moments while writing this chapter when I wanted to walk away from this project, life and people altogether. It took everything in me to complete this first phase because I had to revisit a very painful and difficult place. Completing this book has not been easy. I am trying to write without breaking down. I must gather myself - or should I say gather my life (or what's left of it) while writing.*

The person at my door was standing with her two beautiful girls - one in her hand and the other by her side; she looked as if life had stolen everything from her. From my perspective, I saw death at my door. She was messed up from head to toe; the odor from her body made me sick to my stomach and I was unable to breathe because of the smell. The pain in her spirit reflected in her eyes.

She looked at me with hurting eyes as if to say, *"You're the only hope for my life and my children and I have nowhere else to go".* With no place to call home and no life left in her, I knew that love had to rescue death. No words were spoken and no questions asked, yet I knew something had to be done. She was messed up! The odor of drugs, the smell of sex and the spirit of death encompassed her. While standing, she held her little girls close. Her body so lifeless, frail, and weak; life had taken its toll on her.

I quickly brought them into my home (well, my one- bedroom apartment). I began to assemble one of the greatest medical teams in history. That medical team is called L.O.V.E: Life, Outcome for Victory over Evil. My team was assembled and it took everything in me to make a decision that would change her life and her children's life forever; I had to create a rescue plan.

I couldn't call for help; her family was tired of her, her man had abused her, her pimp had raped her and took all her money, her drug dealer abused her all night and the list goes on. To add to the pain, hurt, disappointment and abuse - her two little girls went through this saga with her. I had to seek the Lord's help to establish this LOVE team. I called for the specialist who was and still is today - the love of God and the love of God within me.

The Bible says in 1 John 3:17; "*...But whoso has this world's goods, and seeth his brother has a need, and shutteth up his bowels of compassion from him, how dwelleth the love of God in him.*" Verse 18 says; "*My little children, let us not love in word, neither in tongue, but let us love in deeds and in truth.*" I didn't have words to say to her - all I could give was LOVE (Life, Outcome, for victory Over Evil). My CPR team was Christ Plan for Reviving.

I started by bringing the children into a safe environment, which I called the love setting. I opened my heart to them by safely placing them in a secure area of my apartment -the 'miracle room', *because miracles happened there*. I wasn't yet saved, but God allowed me to give them a safe place to rest. I loved cooking, so I made my famous meal (breakfast) with all of the love toppings. I now truly understand the term 'soul food'. I was cooking from my soul while death was plaguing her body: the pain ripped my heart. I sought for answers to a lifetime of tragedy, in a world filled with drug addiction, abuse, rape, hurt, disappointments and death. These things take a toll on people and families.

After eating their meals, they were ok. Many thoughts raced through my mind as I pondered the events of the day. All I could hear in the other room was the cry of pain, tragedy, struggle, and death. While love was gaining ground, death was trying to hold its possession - or should I say its position.

My LOVE team was working overtime to defeat the assignments in the atmosphere. I quickly found favor with some peppermints on my living room table for the girls and a little music from the radio being sung by the well-known R&B artist, Baby Face. *Oh yes, Baby Face brought me through some tough relationship moments*. They rested on my sofa while I prepared for the major operation and I certainly needed God's help. With tears in my eyes, I said: "Father in the name of Jesus, help me and save her." The pain I felt was as real as what she was going through. She was dying and the odor from her body filled the room as she begged me for more drugs. *God, what shall I do? I need you for this one!* I had to wash her - yes wash her, because the smell of sex and drugs was taking a toll on us.

I called for love to remove that death spirit from her body, life, and soul. There is a scripture that says in Romans 8:28; *"And we know that all things work together for good to them that love God, to them who are called according to His purpose"*. This means that I was already called. People tend to get this scripture wrong; it says the called according to His purpose, therefore God already had a purpose for me, I just had to choose to follow Him. Another scripture which comes to mind: *"Many are called, but few are chosen."*

I concluded that I was chosen to tell death it would not rule in this person's life, period! Because I knew that the love of God would work it out, I was willing to understand the words *all things* in Romans 8:28. In Greek, this means anything that happens in life; good, bad, happy, or sad - even the injustice, they all work together for good to them who love God and are the called according to His purpose. Purpose means the reason for which something is done, created, and made. The reason for which something exists or is done.

The determination and resolution that resonated in my heart was the word of God. In all of this, my friend had a purpose; *my* purpose was to put an end to death through the love I had in my heart, the hope in my spirit and the victory in my soul. The pain, hurt and disappointment I felt played on my emotions, but God was working it out in love. I quickly moved to the medical issue at hand; her life was at death's door and love was standing at life's door.

Now I understand the scripture in Revelation 3:7 - *"And to the angel of the church in Philadelphia write; These things says He that is holy, He that is true, He that has the key of David, He that*

*openeth, and no man shutteth it, and shutteth no man openeth,
I know thy works: behold I have set before thee an open door
and no man can shut it; for thou hast little strength and has kept
my word, and has not denied my name"* I thank God for that
door which He has set before me. After all, I would not have
had the strength to get the door open, so He had to set it before
me.

There are many things you must understand from this
experience I had many years ago. I was still a sinner, but God
had a purpose for my life. Maybe if someone told me back then
that I would work in God's vineyard - I would have told them
off. But look at me today; I am working under God's direction,
touching lives and de-populating the kingdom of Satan.

I want you to understand the following:

- Many people are crying out for help
- You have love to give
- You can take a bold step and help someone
- Love can overcome anything

Many People Are Crying Out for Help

One thing I learned from my encounter with the woman and
her children, was that there are so many people around us
who are facing the same predicament every day. The only
difference is that in her case, she took a bold step and
appeared at my door with her children seeking help.

Others might not have the faith to do what she did and as such,
they fade away gradually in pain, rejection, and hopelessness.
I know we aren't able to rescue them all, but we can pray that
God will send them helping hands.

Another thing we can do is donate to charity organizations. These organizations were implemented to assist individuals and families experiencing certain situations. Sometimes they provide free health care, clothing, and food items to remote places and different locations. You may not know it, but your small contribution may be a form of your love rescuing someone near death's door.

The most important thing to do is extend a helping hand. Don't look the other way like most people do. Give what you have, which is God's love deposited within you. If I, a sinner at that time can do it - you can do it as well.

You Have Love to Give

You may see yourself as a hard-hearted human being, however I can confidently tell you there is love inside of you to give. God is love and His spirit dwells in all of us, which means there is love lying dormant and waiting for release. You will never know what you are capable of until the time comes or until you are faced with a situation which pulls at your heart strings. All you need to do is open up your heart to those in need. Don't shut your bowel of mercy.

So many would rather look the other way instead of opening their hearts to those in need. Maybe if I saw the woman and her kids on the road, I would have looked the other way. Maybe that's why God brought them directly to my door, so I wouldn't have another choice but to help them.

What I did that day still marvels me. I wasn't aware I could calmly tend to someone in that state, saving them from the hands of death. Actually, we never truly know what we are capable of until something happens, causing us to dig deep within ourselves. You will do more once you realize God has provided all you need.

You Can Take a Bold Step and Help Someone

If I told you it was easy bringing that woman and her children into my home that morning, I would be lying. I had to make a decision and stand on it without wavering. The love of God within me overcame my fears.

I was aware of the responsibilities and legal implications if something happened to her in my house, but what choice did I have? Those hurting eyes of a mom and her two girls were so painful to behold. God decided for me, then used me to save them.

I know it is never easy to 'just do it', allow God to talk to you in that moment of indecision. Being who He is, He will always make the best decision for you. The truth is, everything happens for a reason and if you see yourself in that kind of situation, remember God has a plan.

Love Can Overcome Anything

Love conquers everything. God is love, which means God has the power to change all circumstances. The woman's family had written her off as a drug addict. They may have tried several times to help her to no avail. Friends may have deserted her, thinking she was hopeless - but God said no! All this daughter of Zion needed was love to release her from the dark places of her soul.

While in my house, the lady was still moaning for more drugs because her body was being deprived of the chemicals it was accustomed to receiving. I said a simple prayer with love in my heart and it helped her. Don't ever forget that it might require only a simple act of love to change a terrible situation.

Chapter Two

The Little Boy Under the Bed

I came from a strict holiness background and a home that implemented strong discipline. I was never able to express myself, nor was I shown the affection I believe I needed from those around me. I did not understand what love was all about. My personal definition of love was based upon the tough discipline we experienced.

My perception of love was best described as feelings of fear, difficulties, and challenges. I grew up considering love to be a discipline; a hug was a way of communication instead of a hug as an act of love. As a result, when true love arrived - I was afraid to come from under the bed, not realizing what I thought and experienced about love was entirely wrong.

The little boy under the bed was searching for love, but his quest always ended in hurt, disappointment, lack of loyalty and non-commitment. I never knew how to come from under the bed until one day the right voice, the right sound, the right spirit, and the right person caused me to understand that it was ok to leave my space under the bed. With hands outstretched and in a gentle voice I was told "You can come from under the bed."

Since then, my story has changed. I began to feel the touch of love instead of hearing the sound of "I love you" through tough disciplinary actions carried out in my life. Because of this - I associated love with hurt, pain, unfaithfulness, distrust and lies.

There is so much to be drawn from the story of the boy under the bed. There are many people who have experienced similar situations and are still living under misconceptions of what love entails. Some people find it difficult to come from under the bed, while others are waiting for that voice to draw them out.

Let's consider the following things:

- Who is the child under the bed?
- What kind of love did he experience?
- What was his understanding of love?
- Who brought him out?
- How did it happen?

Who Is the Little Boy Under the Bed?

The little boy under the bed is a lonely boy who lives in fear and distrust, unable to express himself because of his circumstances; a life full of discipline, punishment and hurt. All of these experiences were disguised as love, making it impossible for him to realize that what he was experiencing was not the right kind of love.

There are children who can relate to this story. The type of abuse many have encountered can be quite shocking when exposed. Punishments for small crimes, sexual abuse from respected figures and the perpetual subjection to emotional and physical abuse were all part of the experiences of the little boy under the bed.

The only relief he receives is in his fantasy world, which he created by going under the bed to escape reality. To him, the sound of 'I love you' meant punishment and betrayal, so he preferred to hide from that voice. This describes the boy under the bed.

Children who hide under the bed in search of relief find it difficult to express themselves. They shy away from people because of distrust. They also find it difficult to reach out to others because they believe there is no relief for them in the world.

The sad thing about these children, is that despite the success achieved as adults - the scars and monsters from their past always haunts them. This is why we often find that some have difficulty trusting others. No matter how hard you try to prove your loyalty, your actions are perceived as insincere and too good to be true.

The hurts may fade, but the scars remain. These individuals are mostly reserved; they understand and respond to others in similar situations. If the right person comes into their lives they become more loving and understanding - but if no one rescues them, they will spend the rest of their lives lashing out at others.

What Kind of Love Did He Experience?

Well, I can tell you he didn't experience the right kind of love. If he did, he would not have needed to hide under the bed in an attempt to find refuge and relief.

Love doesn't make you lonely and people don't shy away from the right kind of love. Chastisement in love, is not the same as punishment and cruelty.

Some parents only know how to discipline their children without showing love to them. There must be a clear understanding of your intentions as a parent; you must be able to achieve a balance between punishment and love in order for your children to understand both are for their good.

Growing up in a strict holiness background can be tough on children. Holiness should not be forced on a child, or they will misinterpret it as hatred. When chastising a child, the punishment should be conducive with the crime. When a child misunderstands disciplinary actions, they begin to associate harsh discipline with love - which simply means the acceptable limit has been breached.

 The young boy in our story experienced the wrong kind of love and hid under the bed to shy away from the harsh realities of such love. Even the sound of 'I love you' became something he dreaded – not embraced. A hug meant 'I will deal with you later', instead of 'It's ok, let's talk about it'. True love gives you confidence and brings out the best in you. It is not built on fear, mistrust, betrayal or hurt. It transforms a well-rounded individual from youth to an adult and it also encourages positive impact on people's lives. No one shies away from the right kind of love. We are always searching and wishing someone will show it to us.

Many have experienced love in a negative way, which is why there are so many cases of abuse everywhere. The most hurtful is the abuse which comes from parents to their children. Often when I hear these stories, the pain of this little boy comes alive again.

What Was His Understanding of Love?

 The little boy interpreted love as everything that was wrong. His perception of love was feelings of fear, difficulties and challenges. Who can blame him? If you are subjected to constant humiliation and hardship from the people you expect to protect and love you – whether it's parents, family or friends, wouldn't you end up believing there is no better option?

In this boy's life, love changed from something pure to something evil. The unfortunate thing is that the poor soul didn't even realize someone who could give him what he was yearning for in his spirit. His life seemed dark and uncomfortable and this made him lonely, unable to express himself.

Today, some have the wrong understanding of love due to backgrounds and experiences of betrayals from people who represented a source of love. Hearts have been battered so severely, that whenever the sound of "I love you" is heard, killer instincts appear and strike.

The word of God makes us understand in 1 John 4:18; "*There is no fear in love, but perfect love drives out fear because fear involves punishment. The one who fears has not been perfected in love.*"

I think this verse in the Bible sums it up. If you are living in fear of those who claim to love you, then you are experiencing the wrong kind of love. The Bible has said, "Perfect love drives away fear" When the right kind of love is displayed, the understanding of what love is will automatically change like it did for this boy.

Moreover, the verse continues: *"The one who fears has not been perfected in love."* Based on this particular sentence, it is clear that those who fear, have not been perfected in love. I believe that when true love arrives - fear will vanish and boldness will set in, leading to an ease in self-expression and appreciation.

Who Brought Him Out?

If you ask me, I'd say it was an angel from the Lord. We see them every day in the people around us. Angelic beings move among us and occasionally we experience their presence in our lives. Some are blessed with the hearts of angels and God always use them specifically to pull us out of dire situations.

According to the author of this story, he was able to come out from under the bed when the right voice, the right spirit and the right person told him it was time to come out. It was the right kind of approach, something far different from what he knew. The right voice can mean different things to different people. It may be gentle words of encouragement to a friend suffering from rejection and hurt; words of comfort given to a neighbor in mourning, or just a simple expression of concern to someone hurting. No matter how insignificant it may seem to you, it will go a long way in restoring someone's dignity.

The right spirit denotes the spirit of God, which can only be deposited in individuals who are vessels unto honor. They genuinely care for others and are ready to lend a helping hand to anyone in need. The amazing thing is that you can choose to be that person who reaches out and touches people around you if you wish to be a vessel of love.

We all need to be surrounded by good people. They bring out the best in us; they can chastise us, but not in malicious ways.

They illustrate the perfect love which drives away fear instead of the type that makes you afraid of your own shadow.

To the person reading this story; even if you haven't heard the right voice or met the right person with the spirit to change your misconceptions about love - you don't need to worry. Keep looking forward; that person will surely appear and all those years of hurt and disappointment will definitely disappear.

How Did It Happen?

The right voice spoke, the right spirit communicated with his spirit, then the right person stretched out his hand. The boy grabbed hold and came out from under the bed. It takes the combination of these positive influences in order to convince someone living in loneliness and fear to take that first step forward and change their story.

There are things the little boy did which you can do as well in order to become liberated from this kind of bondage:

- He listened to the voice speaking to him
- He yearned for the right kind of love
- He connected to the right spirit when it arrived
- He removed doubt from his mind
- He grabbed the out-stretched hands
- He took the first step

From henceforth, he experienced what it meant to be loved and cherished. His idea of love changed from fear, disappointment and betrayal, to boldness and security. People under this kind of bondage have difficulties trusting what others say about love.

Even if you've been subjected to this kind of life; the good news is that if you do what this little boy did, you will surely experience the right kind of love which drives away fear as the bible says. If you hear the voice and close your ears, or you find it hard to connect with the spirit - how can you be released from depression? This is a symptom of abused children which remains present through adulthood if healing is not achieved.

If you hear the voice calling you to come out, yet you refuse; how will you become saved? You should listen to the kind voice telling you it is okay to come out or you may miss the opportunity. Finally, you must grab the hand and take the first step from your dark hole. It depends entirely upon you; when 'right' appears to change the wrong that was done, it will be your decision to decide whether you will stay or come out.

The little boy finally felt the type of love he yearned for and his life changed from ugly to beautiful, from depressed to happy and from fright to bravery. You too can have this experience or assist someone with experiencing it as well.

The truth is that real love drives away fear. If you haven't experienced it –wait, for it will surely come when you are ready.

Chapter Three

One Night with The Fiend

It was a one-night affair. A terrible night; I didn't know where I was. I was single, drunk, partying, high on drugs and had sex with various women. As I partied with my friends, we started drinking and I opened myself up to people I didn't know.

As the party progressed, I was introduced to this young lady and we talked about how we had similar issues in our lives, background and experiences. From that moment, I can't quite describe what else happened, except that I woke up the next morning beside a complete stranger. I tried to remember how I ended up spending the night with someone who was only looking for an easy moment and a quick feel.

When she woke up, she smiled and she exclaimed, "Wow! Wow! Wow! I have never experienced anything like this before". I was totally confused. When I asked what she meant, she said that a friend of hers told her about me and had been looking for an opportunity to meet me. Fortunately for her, she got more than she expected, which consisted of wild sex all night.

As we talked, she told me how great I made her feel. When I asked if she enjoyed herself, she said yes and my mind went back to what we talked about in the club. She had just broken up with another guy; thus sleeping with me was her way of getting back at him, so our entire encounter was a one-night fling for her.

I felt stupid and betrayed. Others have landed in similar situations by accident; there are those who deliberately seek one night flings to satisfy the emptiness within and there are others whose only objective is to get revenge on people who hurt them. There are many things to explore and learn from this story.

We can easily understand the following:

- The man was looking for love
- He went to the wrong place
- He let his guard down
- He met the wrong person
- He became a tool to satisfy a selfish interest
- It resulted in betrayal and hurt
- He never found true love

The Man Was Looking for Love

Yes! He was looking for love. The first mistake he made was not realizing the type of love he needed. It is one thing to search for love and another to understand the kind of love you're seeking. You may be surprised, but there are different types of love available for exploration. Amongst them are:

- Storge
- Philia
- Eros
- Agape

Storge: Exists between a parent and his/her child. Every child is expected to have this kind of love for their parents. No matter what situations arise or how angry you are with your parents - there is an unshakable feeling that you can't abandon them, even if you tried. This type of love comes naturally, perhaps from conception to birth. You don't have to search; it is an expected and expressed love. This is why some parents get angry or children revolt when they are not feeling loved. It is also the reason why children find it difficult to abandon their aged parents and the reason parents forgive nearly everything their children do.

Philia; Exists among friends who enjoy a close relationship, such as siblings. This is neither a biological nor organic love. It is a freely-chosen love. It is not mandatory; we have the right to choose our friends and can also choose to drop them if they hurt us. This love allows total control because you decide who to choose as friends -therefore you have the choice to have as many friends as you wish.

Eros; Is a romantic love. It exists between the opposite sex, and can also morph into sex. It exists between husbands and wives and is also the type of love which causes people to say, "I'm in love with him, or her." This type of love can lead to both good and bad. When experienced at the right time, it is wonderful - but when not handled properly, it can transform humans into monsters.

Agape; This is described as the best type of love. It is unconditional and doesn't rely on circumstances. It is one Christian virtue which everyone should achieve. This is the love most people need, but fail to obtain because they don't know how.

The subject of our story failed to realize that what he needed was agape love - not erotic nor philia. If he had taken the time to discern the difference, he wouldn't have ended up more hurt than before.

He Went to The Wrong Place

In the quest to experience agape love, most people fall prey to the erotic type of love believing they can obtain it from the opposite sex. Agape love comes from God and if you want to experience it, you must first go to God; ask for it and He will send it your way through his vessels.

The bible made it clear in 1 John 4:7; "*Beloved, let us love one another because love comes from God. Everyone who loves has been born of God and knows God*" You can only find unconditional love from God because He is love and as such, He loves us unconditionally in return.

Going to a bar and drinking with friends thinking you can find agape love satisfaction is a mistake. Our souls always long for someone to love us totally, without counting our wrongs or loving us only when things are great - then leaving us when the going gets tough. I am here to tell you that you can only find it in the Lord or amongst His sincere followers as the bible states.

Our subject here never understood this; he went to the wrong place seeking inner joy and peace. Most of us are making that same mistake today.

When we feel sad or angry, we look for peace and happiness in the wrong places. At the end of the day, we end up feeling ashamed and emptier than we were before. The right place to find unconditional love is in God's presence.

He Let His Guard Down

Due to his misguided beliefs, he thought one night among friends would alleviate his pains and loneliness. Because he thought he was in the right place, he allowed the devil to enter and lead him further astray. Giving in to the rhythm of the moment; he drank, smoked, laughed and became intoxicated to the extent he felt at home amidst strangers.

According to the scriptures in 1 Corinthians 10:12, "*Wherefore let him that thinketh he standeth take heed lest he falls.*" At the point when you think you have made the right decisions in life - St. Paul admonishes that you should be careful or else, you may fall. Letting his guard down enabled the devil to mislead him.

Drinking and partying wildly is never a good thing. When alcohol controls a man, he becomes its slave. He will go where he is pushed and do what he is told. Sometimes I wonder why people subject themselves to such humiliations by an unknown force, only to feel ashamed at the end of the day. Why indulge in something that will dehumanize you and turn you into a subject of caricature?

He Met the Wrong People

The places where you choose to hang out will determine the type of people you meet. He was looking for something pure in the wrong place and ended up meeting the wrong people. The lady he went home with was introduced to him by someone else. The friends you keep will also play a significant role regarding where you go and the people you encounter.

His friends were wrong. They took him to the wrong place and introduced him to the wrong woman who finished the whole saga. No one can offer what they don't have. How can I give you what I don't know or have? If you want true love and connect with someone who has never experienced love, what can you gain? Nothing, I tell you.

If you desire the unconditional love that comes from God, you must search amongst His real children. Those who have experienced and know what it means to love unconditionally; because of this, they can quickly and selflessly give to others. As in John 3:16; *"For God so loved the world, that He gave His only begotten son"*.

Stop looking for real love from people who don't know what it is or what it feels like. Go to the right people and you will be happy you did.

He Became a Tool to Satisfy a Selfish Interest

Do you know what's funny? When you fall into the hands of the wrong people, they will selfishly use you. In 1 Corinthians chapter 13, the Bible makes us understand that love doesn't seek its own. This apparently means that true love is never selfish; it puts others first and will never use someone else for its interests.

The gentleman in this story was used as a tool to satisfy someone's deflated ego. She was dumped and in order to feel valued, she used the next available, unsuspecting individual to make herself feel like a queen. She didn't care how the other person felt - she was only concerned about her feelings.

You can only be used when you let your guard down. When you don't have control of your senses, you land in places where you never desired and will become a tool in the hands of selfish individuals who don't care about you. What started as a quest for joy, resulted in the seeker becoming prey because he let his guard down with the wrong people.

It Resulted in Betrayal and Hurt

There will always be a rude awakening to reality. Dreams just don't last forever. No matter how intoxicated you are, a moment of clarity comes and you will remember how foolish and gullible you were in the hands of the devil. I wonder, who would feel elated when they finally realize they have been used and dumped? No one. When reality sets in, the taste of betrayal and hurt is all that is left in your mouth. Selfish people use and dump others. When you fall into their net, you will understand what betrayal means. If you have selfish friends, they will only be there when you are able to meet their needs; as soon as an opportunity presents itself and you aren't able to meet their needs, you will be replaced immediately.

Unfortunately, most people who experience betrayal are those who are sincere in their relationships. The subject in our story may have been hoping for something better after the night he spent with the stranger. He may have thought, "well since we went this far, we might as well take it further and see where it will lead us..." False expectations! He was just a tool and when his usefulness expired, he was dumped ruthlessly.

Feeling disappointed and betrayed, he could only bow his head in regret. Don't allow yourself to be exposed to the devil; he will destroy your life. Betrayal can be heart- wrenching and makes you feel worthless and abandoned. Do what is right for you today and avoid hurt.

He Never Found the True Love

It's a pity he never got what he truly wanted, which was true love. He had a need but didn't know what it was. The only thing that can satisfy you and bring you into the realm of inner peace and joy, is *true* love. Most people desire it, but miss it because they search in the wrong places from the wrong people.

The Bible tells us that God is love and in Him, you can find unconditional love. It was virtually impossible for the author of this story to receive love in the places where he was searching. Unfortunately, at that point in his life he didn't get what he wanted. He got love, but the wrong type known for bad results if mishandled.

Let us bear in mind today that the only love which can bring inner peace and joy is agape love. It is an unconditional love which is not based on situational changes. It comes from God and can be found amongst those who have experienced the same type of love. In your search, go only to the right places and prevent falling into the hands of the devil and his agents. True love lasts for eternity.

Chapter Four

Love; The Roller Coaster Ride
(My First Love)

I was 19 years old and for the first time in my life I believed in my heart that I was in love. She was 16 years old. A beautiful dark-skinned girl with the body of a stallion. We met at my place of employment and began to talk and after few minutes, I got her number.

We lost contact for some time but later reconnected and that was when the roller coaster-ride of love began. In retrospect, I really believed what we had was true love. My feelings for her were so strong; I was ready and willing to give her all the positive things life had to offer. She had my heart on a platter.

During this time period, I was a well-known State and Regional tennis player with many scholarships and opportunities. However, my love and passion for her were so intense - I forgot about what was important. The relationship took me to levels I never thought I would reach; crying, hurting, and almost losing my mind.

When the 1st child came, I thought I would have the perfect family; a lifetime of bliss for my family. Well, it didn't work out as planned, because she moved away and took my son. From that moment the ride intensified; I was on the brink of losing it. It broke my heart to be separated from my child. I wanted to be a faithful and loving father, but the opportunity was stripped away from me.

The distance between us made it difficult to be with her and my son. Financial hardship made it nearly impossible. I tried really hard to hang in there - but just 24 hours to our wedding, things shifted for the worse: the wedding was called off. I mean, the devastation literally ripped me apart. After everything I did, the dream of having a family dimmed before my eyes. Having no other option, I continued to be the best father I could.

Love can indeed become a roller coaster ride if you land on the wrong side. I don't want to use the term 'false love,' because love is never wrong - however you can have the wrong interpretation of love for sure. Love is never wrong. If God is love and God is never wrong - how can there be a wrong love? What we have is a wrong interpretation of love disguised by infatuation.

Infatuation causes many to become disgusted with the idea of true love because it resulted in pain. A crush can make you feel as if you are in love and will take you on a roller coaster ride. There are several things to explore from this example: where did things go wrong?

- It was not the right age
- It was not love
- Lust and passion were the focus
- The weight of responsibility too heavy
- The feelings were one-sided
- It was not the right time

It Was Not the Right Age

The boy and girl in the story were young; 19 and 16 years old. They were both teenagers who should have been under an adult's guidance. Trying to be an adult prematurely can lead to misfortune. As teenagers, we believe what we feel is true love and that it will last forever. The idea of 'happily ever after' has been a constant thrill for every teenager.

We often misinterpret infatuation for love as teenagers and we tend to believe the feelings will last forever. Unfortunately, it is never as expected and planned. The subjects in our story were too young; they had youthful exuberance flowing through them. It happens to many teenagers and it takes adult intervention to calm things down. Many mistakes made by teenagers often come back to haunt them. Parents should be very observant when their children fall in 'so called love'. When it begins to happen, parents should help their children understand that the feeling is not love and the importance of taking it easy to avoid making mistakes.

It Was Not Love

It is quite apparent that what the writer experienced was not love. Love can be intense and goes very deep. It doesn't happen instantaneously, but develops gradually over time. Based on this story, everything happened so quickly that his experience made him feel as if he were on a rollercoaster. Love does not fade, but grows stronger, deeper and more powerful over time.

From what we see, their love dissipated instead of growing. They could not resolve their issues which led to separation.

True love is more than just physical attraction. He never took the time to find out about the 'real her'. Besides physical beauty - virtues such as patience, understanding and endurance are what sustain love in a relationship. Blinded by her physique, he neglected the other important factors and made a huge mistake in his life.

Love is never selfish; it always considers the feelings of others. The young girl never thought about how the boy would feel if she took away his son. In marriages today, spouses hurt each other selfishly when they make decisions that devastate their partners. True love will always consider how the other person feels and how battered one's heart would be if the wrong decision or action transpires.

If you are in this type of relationship; you are neither giving nor receiving true love and if nothing changes, you will end up in misery.

The Focus Was Lust

Because of their age and misinterpreted feelings, the focus of the entire relationship was lust. They jumped into sexual relations without thinking about consequences. That's right; every action has a consequence. Adults know this, however teenagers fail to understand the concept.

Lust is a force that can overcome almost anyone. It focuses on the physical, not the internal. The couple never had time to nurture the relationship and as such, missed out on true love.

Lust always ends as quickly as it starts and leaves its prey miserable, hurt and abandoned. Lust routinely begins as a good feeling, but ends badly.

The next time you feel like you are riding a roller coaster of emotions for someone, take a deep breath and return to reality or else you will be rudely awakened.

The Weight of Responsibility Was Too Heavy

True love is characterized by patience, endurance and long-suffering. In this story, the responsibility of having a child became difficult and as a result, it weighed heavily on their feelings.

Having a child at such a young age is not a joke. I have witnessed adults run away from relationships because their partners became pregnant. After the baby was born, things became more than they could handle. Even though they managed for a while, the girl finally moved in with her parents and enrolled in school.

Imagine being sixteen years old and carrying a child whose father is also a teen. Without the support of an adult, the situation would be difficult to survive. This is not a new scenario in today's society; many teenagers have given up their dreams for a better life, because they fell into the trap of infatuation instead of true love.

When love appears, it brings out the best in you; it doesn't leave you in a dark place, but instead helps you achieve all that you can.

Parents today should make it clear to teenagers that every action has its consequences and depending upon the severity of the act, those involved will always lose. Meaningless relationships and careless sex in the name of love never win.

The Feeling Was One-Sided

The feelings were not mutual; the boy wished to build a family, but the girl had different intentions. Not sharing mutual feelings caused the young man to suffer during the span of the relationship. He sacrificed a great deal, yet it was not enough because his partner did not feel the same way.

We can say that age is the primary reason for this dilemma, yet we have adults who experience the very same thing in relationships. One-sided love is a terrible experience and causes one to feel inadequate and undesirable. Those who have experienced it can relate. When love is mutual, both partners have a better chance of making things work.

There is no reason to remain in a relationship where you are making all the sacrifices. Often in the beginning, it may seem easy - but with time, things will take its toll. Relationships are for adults - not teenagers, because maturity will assist a person in identifying when love is one-sided.

True love binds two people together in oneness. I say this because when one feels that unconditional love known as Agape love - romance naturally ensues and finally leads to marriage.

Most marriages today result in divorce, most likely because things began as a roller coaster ride and led to a wedding. Both parties probably did not take time to understand that what sustains a marriage is not the initial passion - but the Godly kind of love, which is unconditional.

After a while in the marriage, couples start noticing their numerous differences which were not visible to the eyes of passion. Before anyone realizes there is a problem in paradise, divorce papers are signed. Sometimes, I feel angry in my spirit with the mockery that even Believers are making of the institution ordained by God in the Garden of Eden.

People are not patient enough to understand that unless you love the way God loves, you will never succeed in the act of love. We are talking about all four types of love; Philia, Storge, Eros and Agape. The faster we realize that God must be at our center, the easier it will be to engage in the right kind of love that doesn't leave us battered and disillusioned.

It Was Not the Right Time

According to the book of Ecclesiastics 3:1- "*To everything, there is a season, and a time to every purpose under the heaven.*" Yes! There is a time for everything and when you don't wait for the right moment for your purpose, nature will drag you back to your starting point.

The couple in this story started something prematurely and ended up with nothing. Teenagers who engage in pre-marital sex jump the gun.

Eros type of love is not for kids and the Bible also mentions this when it admonishes us in 1Timothy 2:22 - says, "*Flee also youthful lusts: but follow righteousness, faith, charity, peace, with them that call on the Lord out of a pure heart.*"

In addition to what the Bible says, many health experts repeatedly speak on the dangers of pre-marital sex. It can lead to the following:

- Unwanted pregnancy
- Sexually-transmitted diseases
- HIV and AIDS

- Emotional trauma
- Depression
- Personality disorder
- Death through abortion

Another note-worthy danger is the potential negative impact to one's future. The young man was a professional tennis player with several scholarship offers on the table. When he engaged in that emotional roller coaster ride, he abandoned his dreams due to an unplanned pregnancy and the pursuit of premature family life.

The young lady had dreams as well, but she was burdened by the responsibility of taking care of a baby at a tender age. All her plans for a bright future flew out of the window the moment she made the wrong decision. No wonder she was unable to continue the relationship, because her infatuation automatically transformed to disappointment, anger, and frustration.

Many teenagers altered the course of their destinies because they pursued the right thing at the wrong time. There is a time for true love, marriage, and family. You cannot jump from step one to step five and still believe you will be okay. If you wait for a mature age, you will thoroughly enjoy everything love has to offer.

The first step to Erotic love is Agape. When you can love God and love your neighbor as yourself - then it becomes easy to love your spouse unconditionally. Without knowing the meaning of sacrificial love, how can you survive in a relationship filled with sacrifices? If you want love to work out for you, you must understand the sacrificial love which comes from God.

Chapter Five

LUST; THE ROLLER COASTER RIDE
"When the atmosphere shifted…"

After concluding that I would never experience what I desired from the encounter with my first love, I escaped into a life of lust, partying, stripping, drinking, drugs and whatever destructive habit I could partake. It was a ride that impacted my life and the relationships which followed. I became addicted to lust and more lust, in an attempt to escape love.

After the turmoil experienced by misinterpreting infatuation as love, the young man decided he would never have anything to do with love again. Deeply hurt by the disappointment and betrayal he experienced with his child's mother, he chose to seek revenge on every lady he met. Instead of understanding his mistakes, he proceeded to make more by living a life of lust.

There is much to learn from this story. Many have experienced the same issues and many are still making the same mistakes. He had a one-time experience of hurt and decided that love was for the weak-hearted; therefore, he wanted to engage love on his terms.

I have encountered many people who will argue from morning until night in an attempt to prove that true love doesn't exist. I was among those same people, before I gave my life to Christ and discovered I was making a huge mistake.

Often you will hear these people say:

"If you insist that love exists, why are marriages breaking up?"

"How is it that couples are always unfaithful to each other if love is faithful?"

"Why do people who love each other end up hurting themselves?"

I tell you, the list goes on and on and if you don't know what you believe - you may end up believing their truth of love not existing. True love does exist because we have already proven that God is love. So if God exists, love exists as well.

Let's explore the young man's mistakes:

- He made a wrong assumption
- He chose a bad alternative
- He entered into a life of lust
- He distanced himself from true love
- He didn't find satisfaction

He Made Wrong Assumptions

The first mistake he made was assuming his first encounter was true love. True love doesn't leave you disillusioned. It is love that has its foundation rooted in God. Every child of God who experiences through love can testify it is the best thing that could ever happen.

It all started with God when the Bible told us in John 3:16, "*For God so loved the world that He gave His only begotten son*" God loved His creation and He sacrificed the one thing He loved, which was His only begotten son. True love is rooted in God and is sacrificial in nature.

Personally, I believe true love is reserved for true children of God because they know what it means to say "I love you" to their Heavenly Father. The young man never experienced true love, however he assumed he did and that it was a failure.

The second assumption he made was believing that he would never experience true love in his life. Given that his initial experience was wrong simply meant that he didn't experience love at all. Those who have been badly hurt while giving love to others become extremely cautious and guarded when required to open their hearts.

God gives multiple chances; He forgives His children of their sins and restores what was lost. He does this repeatedly. Instead of thinking that love will never come again, pray and ask God to deposit His love upon you through individuals who will demonstrate what love means. Don't conclude that it's over and not deserved. As long as you give your life to the giver of true love and remain as His child, you are entitled to a second chance at true love whether in friendship, family or marriage.

He Was Afraid of Rejection

The young man was terrified of love in fear of rejection. The truth is we all want to open our hearts freely, but we want assurance that when we do, we will be accepted - not rejected. We have heard the saying 'once bitten, twice shy'; this is true because if you open your heart to someone and they hurt you, you will naturally find it difficult to open yourself again.

Because of the risk involved, we don't admit the truth that we are all in dire need of love. We hold on to what appears to be easier at the moment while we pretend as if we don't care. The same thing happened to our subject. The hurt he experienced caused him to close his heart the second time around.

Many people have experienced the same things and responded in the same manner. Some desire love - but because of the fear of rejection, they pretend as if they are okay, while hurting deep inside. The fear of being rejected, ridiculed or being abandoned prevents them from seeking love. The truth of the matter is that when you meet the right people, opening your heart is not a risk. They have what you need and are ready to give.

True love does not ridicule; it covers weaknesses and enables a person to be their best. Instead of pretending and engaging in self-destructive behaviors, look out for God's children and receive them. Instead of hurting you, they will find a way to assist and make you a better person so that true love can enter.

He Chose the Wrong Alternative

Believing true love would never cross his path, the young man in our story decided the best thing to do was close his heart and hurt as many people as possible. This is so unfortunate because people with this same belief miss the opportunity of being loved properly. Selfish decisions cause people to treat the opposite sex solely as tools of sexual satisfaction - nothing more. When they finally realize the path of destruction they've created, it's almost impossible to find friends who remain.

He Entered a Life of Lust

You can't replace love with lust or you'll fall into a deep pit dug by the devil to trap your soul. Choosing to hurt and use others is as detrimental as burning yourself with fire. While you may have been disillusioned by your first love experience; inflicting emotional pain does not remove your own misery or improve your life. Once true love occurs, it can never be replaced by hurting others.

The young man lived a lustful life in order to relieve his personal pain. His life became characterized by partying, stripping, drinking, drugs and other destructive acts which all negatively impacted his future. The manner in which he lived was a fast track to death. Imagine a person destroying himself because he could not get what he wanted. Who does that? Only little children throwing tantrums in an attempt to get their wishes fulfilled act that way. How can an adult engage in such nonsense in the name of disappointment?

Lust and fleshly desires are of the devil. How can you embrace drinking as a substitute for love? This is the first step to losing your self-worth. Partying; the beginning of a bleak future. Drugs: the foundation for madness. Sex with multiple partners; the perfect invitation to death. All these tendencies come from the devil which is why Paul admonishes us to flee youthful lust because therein lies destruction.

Love is always the best option. Replacing it with lust leads to multiple mistakes which could potentially cause you to become a failure forever unless saved by God.

He Moved Farther Away from True Love

There is no unrighteousness in God, He is the source of true love. When you invite the devil into your heart - in essence, you have made it clear that you no longer have space for true love. Right now, you may feel that you will never experience true love again and so it is best to live without it – but that is far from the truth! Do you know why? God is paying attention to every detail of your life.

The young man invited the devil into his life by living recklessly in sin - therefore, God moved away from him. The deeper he submerged himself in sin, the farther away he moved from true love. There is no communication between darkness and light. Either you choose God, or you choose mammon. Just remember that choosing God means accepting true love; your life is nothing without him.

The devil is always seeking ways to destroy you. He has no love in his heart and running to him is like willingly going to hell. Regardless of your previous experiences, you have a story to tell. Don't justify your actions and certainly do not sacrifice your chances of finding true love in God. Perhaps you don't know that love is beautiful and makes things perfect.

He Didn't Find Satisfaction

The most painful thing about sin is that it doesn't offer anything, but takes more than you bargained to give. The satisfaction in drugs and alcohol does not last long. It makes you feel high at that moment, then shocks you with a reality never expected. The Bible says in Proverbs 20:1 – "*Wine is a mocker, strong drink is raging: and whosoever is deceived thereby is not wise.*"

Alcohol and drugs reduce you to foolery and control you to the point of destruction, but will never satisfy you. Another example from the scripture is in Genesis 9:21 *"He drank of the wine and became drunk, and uncovered himself inside his tent"* Now, how can you find satisfaction in something that reduces you to foolishness?

Fornication and adultery are other things which never satisfies. Unless God is showing you His divine mercy - you could become infected with a serious disease. HIV/AIDS is one of the most dreaded diseases of our time. I recently heard about a young lady who had several things going for her, but she acquired the HIV virus. From that moment forward, her life and future became sad and bleak.

She stayed alive for some years while hoping for redemption from God: she turned to God and chose to serve Him. A few days ago, I learned of her passing.

The people who visited her from the church could not believe how emaciated and tiny she had become. The news of her death prompted a comment from someone close which touched me. He said, "Just a few minutes of enjoyment rendered this young lady sad until her death". Being reckless in the search of satisfaction can render you miserable for the rest of your life. Stop trying to find joy in things that will do more harm than good to your life. Remember that every good thing comes from God alone.

Chapter Six

Hurt Made Me Discriminate Against Love

I was so badly hurt from my journey in lust, it led to a cascade of bad choices. I ended up getting into relationships where the other person would love me, however I was unable to reciprocate love in return. Most of these relationships were based upon the fulfillment I received from them.

Being hurt by the one you love is something no one wants to experience. In addition to the fact that it is extremely painful - many questions are left unanswered. The young man found hurt instead of love. His first crush resulted in bitterness, so he lived life in the pain of his experience. His lustful life caused even more hurt and he therefore chose to believe that love was nonexistent. He encountered several individuals who were ready to offer love, but his heart was already closed. He only desired sexual satisfaction and personal gain.

This lifestyle led to doom - not redemption, however there were factors responsible for his empty life:

- He was hurt
- He wanted nothing to do with love
- He became a sex addict
- He hurt people
- He lost several opportunities to love

Many have passed through these stages in life. Some chose the path to God and have received the true love which comes from Him alone. There are others who never opened their hearts to salvation because they believed they understood it all and as such, could liberate themselves.

If you are presently living a life similar to the young man's, it is time for you to open your heart to God and stop hurting. When you receive Christ as the Bible says in 1Corinthians 5:17, "...*you become a new creature; old things are pass away, and behold all things have become new again*". The entrance of the Holy Spirit into your heart will change your life.

Let's discuss relevant facts from the experience.

He Was Hurt

The young man had difficulty since childhood. Being deprived of true love while growing up, he lived in loneliness and fear. After the disappointment and betrayal following his experience at 19 - he chose lust over love, which caused more hurt due to poor choices. After this experience, his self-esteem received a massive blow and in an attempt to conceal his true feelings, he lashed out at others.

To tell the truth, we all hate rejection. It sucks. It makes one feel insecure, useless and unattractive. If you don't know how to handle rejection, you will either withdraw totally or hurt others. As humans, we have this innate need to feel important, recognized and appreciated by others. When the situation doesn't favor us in this manner, we tend to feel betrayed and abandoned.

Rejection is a part of life and there is nothing we can do except learn how to handle it when it occurs. When rejected or betrayed - a person feels hurt, especially when their intentions were good. The worst feeling is when you have done everything possible, but you still get hurt. When you sacrifice much - yet your efforts go unappreciated, that really hurts.

As we journey through life, we can only pray that God sends the right people into our lives who will appreciate us. Unfortunately for the young man, he wasn't patient enough to wait for the right person and acted out from a place of pain. Hurting others left him feeling disgusted with himself.

He Wanted Nothing to Do with Love Again

After being hurt and not wanting love anymore, the young man lived a carefree life. I cannot say I blame him because opening your heart after being hurt is never easy. His high expectation for love and a family was shattered at a tender age, something he was unable to forget quickly.

He later met people who were eager to show him love, but his heart was closed. Imagine how scared he was when someone tried to confess their love. It was easier to hear someone say "I love you" than to risk loving them and being rejected. His first love did a number on him. The experience left him battered and bitter. Despite the heartbreak however, life must go on: love cannot compete with hate.

Today, many have closed their hearts to love and would rather engage in sex than love. Use them and dump them has become a theme which is followed because it is easier than falling in love and risk being hurt. Instead of settling down with one person, they would rather to 'play the field'.

When a person decides they don't want love, they are really deceiving themselves because love is the only thing which can heal and restore. You cannot discriminate against love. God will always try to win you back. Knowing that you are hurt, He is ready to send the right people to assist in the healing of your wounds and the restoration of your joy. So whether it's wanted or not, true love will always locate those in need.

No matter how stubborn we are, we will never be bigger than our maker - so don't fight true love. It is like fighting God. Just trust Him, He knows the right thing for you. He alone can align you with the right people who will come into your life and make you a better person.

He Became a Sex Addict

This is the alternative people often embrace. Instead of going to God and seeking His help, the young man gave in to his fleshly desires and slept around with several women. According to the young man, "Most of these relationships were based on just sex and what he could get from the other person."

Sometimes I hear the phrase 'friends with benefits' and I often wonder why people would use each other as a tool for sexual satisfaction and nothing more.

Both parties use each other when there is a need and interestingly enough they go their way until the next time they need to 'scratch an itch'. Such emotional detachment is of the devil. The Bible says clearly in Romans chapter 12:1, "*I beseech you, therefore, brethren, by the mercies of God, that you present your bodies a living sacrifice, holy, acceptable to God which is your reasonable service.*"

The second verse to consider is 1 Corinthians 6:18-20, "*Flee from sexual immorality. Every other sin a man can commit is outside his body, but he who sins sexually against his body. Do you not know that your body is a temple of the Holy Spirit who is in you, whom you have received from God? You are not your own; you were bought with a price. Therefore glorify God with your body*".

How can someone who wishes to experience true love embrace sex as a substitute? You are truly pushing away any chance of love and defiling your body - where the Spirit of God is supposed to dwell. A life full of sexual immorality will never experience true love. True love will always elude those who indulge in such a lifestyle if they don't stop.

He Hurt Many People

"I used them for my personal gain."

I know there is no excuse for hurting others, but an old adage says it clearly: 'hurting people hurt people'. Those who experienced emotional pain tend to inflict their pain on others.

This is why sexually-abused children become abusers as adults and children of alcoholic parents tend to repeat that behavior upon their own family.

The young man was hurt, so he began hurting as many people as he could. Many of the women he crossed paths with were seen as sexual toys and tools for personal gain. One after the other, he used them and left them because he did not know how to deal with the pain and void inside.

His actions are similar to those of many people in our society today. Hurting people tend to do the following:

- They transfer their anger onto close friends and family

- Every word heard is painful
- They interpret actions through their pain
- They justify their actions by playing the victim
- They push others away and lash out when someone leaves them
- They tend to be depressed and frustrated
- They are absorbed in pain, forgetting their actions hurt others

These characteristics are common among hurt people. They usually don't plan to hurt others, but things generally end that way. Only the touch of God can bring healing and forgiveness. Instead of harboring hurt and deep pain - let it go, or more problems will be created in our society. When we are hurt, we should lean towards God so that we can be set free.

He Lost Several Opportunities to Love

According to the story, many people reached out in love - some were rejected, while others were disappointed. While hurting others, you never realize when you have lost the one person who could've made a positive impact on your life. Everyone you meet may not allow you to hurt them at will. People who work with the spirit of God can discern a deceitful spirit from afar and will run the opposite way.

When hurt dominates a person's life, bitterness appears and the Spirit of God will depart. The worst thing that can happen is to operate under the influence of the devil. Instead of being liberated, he/she will be dragged to hell. The devil knows that the heart is where all thoughts emanate. He attacks God's children with emotional pain so he can occupy their hearts with darkness. He will always remind you of your hurt so that you become angrier each day and commit more mayhem.

Besides becoming disconnected with the spirit of God, you will experience loneliness because you tend to push people away. When people discover you are intolerant of them, they won't have anything to do with you. By the time you realize what you have done, your life is empty. Your close friends will depart or keep their distance.

The good news is that there is hope for people who have been betrayed or who are suffering. The first thing to do is realize you are suffering from hurt – but are not damaged. Your life is not done. When you come to this realization, you will become open to the process of healing and restoration.

To heal your emotions, you must reach out to God in prayer for healing and seek His presence. He is a loving father who is always ready to heal His children at all times. One recommendation is to find a trustworthy man or woman of God and discuss your hurt and pain. You cannot do it alone, that's for sure. God will send His children around you to encourage, strengthen and surround you with love. When this is done, you will be free to repair the damaged relationships and reconcile with those you've hurt.

We cannot discriminate against love. We all need someone to connect with. No matter how far you run - at some point, you will regret those acts of recklessness that pushed people away.

Chapter Seven

The Love Department

Love has many powerful overtones. There is a love department existing in every human life. It's similar to purchasing items in a department store. In order to enter the love department of another human - one must be able to afford that person's love items. One must be able to understand and meet all conditions before they can purchase anything from your store.

There are no price tags in the love department, so bargaining with love items is not an option. There are no negotiations, no discounts and absolutely no sales in the love department. When you arrive at the love department in your life - everything you see is priceless, everything you get is expensive and everything you ask for is needed.

There are no receipts and no return of items in the love department. Personally, the value of items in my love department is unmeasurable and you will always desire more love; this is because all items in the love department are priceless and the value is the 'love secret'. You're probably wondering 'What does he mean by the items are priceless and the value is the love secret'? Well, let me explain.

Love Department

The simplest illustration to use in describing the love department, is to compare it to a department store. A department store as we all know, is a large retail establishment which has different goods organized into separate departments that operate under the same building and control. There are characteristics of a department store to outline:

- They offer a variety of goods
- They have small, independent departments
- They are centrally-managed and controlled
- Each department offers excellent service
- You can find everything needed

The love department is like a departmental store with several facets operating in oneness to give what you need and provides a wholesome experience. When you penetrate someone's love department, you will most likely remain. Love has multiple products to offer necessary for human existence.

We go to the love department store to shop whenever there is a need to be met, hoping we will receive what we are searching for. We expect to find something in the love department of our close friends, families and spouses. When we fail to receive what is expected, we feel disappointed and betrayed. Maybe you didn't know that when you expect someone to be kind, you are shopping for kindness in his/her love department store.

One thing to also note is that both the seeker and the person being sought has a love department. We only open up to those who have met our requirements or who have shown that they value who and what we are. No one can easily enter someone's department unless the door is opened.

Have you ever wondered why it's easier to show love to some people, while others bring out the worst in you? The people you are open to are those who have touched you in a positive way – maybe they opened their hearts to you or recognized your worth. When you feel loved, it becomes difficult to close your heart to the other person.

Items in the Department

Just like a department store, our love department has a variety of goods to offer and each are priceless. The products available in the love department are:

- Patience
- Kindness
- Selflessness
- Humility
- Forgiveness
- Perseverance
- Trust
- Protection
- Hope
- Loyalty

These are the characteristics of love as listed in 1 Corinthians chapter 13:4-8 and the same items found in the love department as well. These items cannot be quantified, and as such, they have no price tag. If you can't measure something, how can you attach a price? Let's review their meaning and why they are needed.

Patience; is the ability to accept or tolerate delay or trouble without getting angry or upset when things don't go the way expected. People with patience can tolerate mistakes, delays and problems without running away or assigning blame. This is the reason we find it easier to tolerate the flaws of those we sincerely love.

Kindness; this is the ability to be generous, considerate, and spontaneous - showing goodwill to others no matter the situation. Love without giving is a fallacy. Giving is the expression of love; it is both tangible and intangible goods.

Selflessness; this is the ability to show more concern for the needs and feelings of others before yours. The opposite is called selfishness. When you love someone, you consider their feelings first before your own.

Humility; the act of showing respect and regards to others while having a modest or low view of your importance. You don't put down the person you love. Instead, you try to showcase them before others.

Forgiveness; the act of pardoning someone who offends you and forgetting the crime as well. You let go of vengeful emotions and still wish the other person well. Hard right? It takes the actual love from God to forgive and forget a stab in the back.

Perseverance; the ability to continue doing something, no matter the challenges and difficulties encountered. While loving people, there are many things that will discourage you. What can you do except hang in there?

Trust; the ability to firmly believe in what someone says or in the reliability of someone else. It is like having an unshakeable confidence in someone's ability, actions or words.

Protection; the capacity to keep someone safe from danger. You can't bear to see someone you love in pain. If possible, you will offer to take their pain.

Hope; the feeling that something good will inevitably happen. No matter the situation, you will always expect good from your loved ones.

Loyalty; a sense of duty and a devoted attachment to someone else, no matter what others say or do.

These items found in the love department cannot be quantified and will never have a price tag. If you want to access to the - you must show merit not by money, but through priceless actions as well. To ask if we need them is an understatement. We can't survive without them and as a result, we become disappointed when they are not received.

Cost of Love

If you put a price on love, it means that you are attaching a price to something priceless from your love department. Well, this is not love because the cost of love is intangible and priceless. The first cost of love can be found in John 3:16, "*For God so loved the world that He gave his only begotten son*" God loved us and He gave something "His only begotten son" something priceless - no cost; is God's love for you and me.

Another cost of love in the Bible is in Genesis 22:2 "*God commanded, Take your son, your only son, Isaac, whom you love, and go to the region of Moriah. Sacrifice him there as a burnt offering"* When Abraham heard this, he did not hesitate because of his love for God. *"Early the next morning Abraham got up and saddled his donkey. He took with him two of his servants and his son Isaac. When he had cut enough wood for the burnt offering, he set out for the place God had told him about..."* Abraham even lied to his son Isaac in order to obey God's commandment.

Another example was the love which existed between David and Jonathan. Jonathan, who was Saul's son, knew Saul was trying to kill David - yet his love for David caused him to betray his flesh and blood and saved David. Jonathan knew that he would lose the favor of his father, but he still protected his friend whom he loved so much. The love that David had for Jonathan allowed him to trust him completely without any fear of betrayal.

Some people will tell you that love does not cost a thing, however this is a lie. Love will cost you many things which can never be quantified. Its cost is intangible and will leave a gap in your being. Love means sacrifice. Now that you have seen all the items people look for in your love department, can you tell me which of these items would be easy to give? None, I tell you. Try forgiving someone who killed your son and still wish them well - or try to be kind to someone who caused you to lose your job. None of these items are easy display during difficult circumstances.

Love demands the most precious things. This is why the Bible calls it unconditional and sacrificial. The things you sacrifice will always be precious and priceless. If you are not ready to sacrifice, you are not ready to love.

Lust Has a Price Tag

Lust is a luxury with a price tag. It could cost you heartache, hard times, pain and possibly a heart attack. Lust can render you useless by taking all of your money.

For every lustful desire, there is a monetary involvement. If you want sexual satisfaction, you either pay for a prostitute or maintain a friend with benefits. Lust comes with a price tag and money is always required to satisfy its desires. Lust may inflict so much pain, it could possibly lead to a heart attack. What is a heart attack? According to the National Heart Lung and Blood Institute: "A heart attack occurs when the flow of oxygen-rich blood to a section of heart muscle suddenly becomes blocked and the heart cannot receive oxygen. If blood flow isn't restored quickly, that section of the heart muscle begins to die." Many never survive a heart attack.

Lust can also be used as a bargaining chip, used as a reward or as a punishment. You don't obtain what you want without losing something in return and that 'something' could eventually be your life. The worst thing about lust is that it demands you to spend, but you never receive lasting satisfaction. This means that the price of lust is higher than the value it offers.

This is where love and lust differ. The more value you offer in love - the more value you get out of love.

The Love Secret

I am going to use a Bible verse to share the secret of love. Mathew 7:12 states; "*So whatever you wish that others would do to you, do also to them, for this is the Law and the Prophets.*" This is it: give to others what you expect them to give you. The more you value others, the more they will value you. The more love you show to others - the more love you will receive in return.

Love is sacrificial in nature. How can you expect others to sacrifice for you when you don't give anything? It must first come from you before others are drawn to you. Wanting to be loved but not willing to give love is like reaping where you did not sow. The cost of love is meant to be shared by two people who express their love for each other. When one party make all the sacrifices, eventually they will revolt and lose interest entirely.

If at all possible, it is better to give before someone gives to you. God showed it first by giving His son when we did not deserve it and we still find it difficult to love Him the way He requires.

In summary, everyone has a love department. It can only be opened when one chooses to love. Understanding how priceless the items are in your department will allow you to open yourself to the right person. Love has no price tag, but it has a high cost. Unlike lust which has a price tag attached - love adds value to its subjects.

Love is sacrificial and requires one to be selfless. In order to achieve all the benefits of love, it must be a shared effort between two individuals willing to explore the love department for a lifetime.

Chapter Eight

Oracle of love

I want to share my heart with you today. There is a love I have yet to touch, feel and experience in my life. It lies within the innermost part of my mind, heart and soul. Yes, I have experienced love - however, my destiny has not yet encountered this specific love. If I had experienced this specific love, I would not keep searching for someone or something to fulfill Laron Matthews. To complete my destiny, the Bible says; "*...In me dwell no good thing that is in my flesh,*" Romans: 7:18 KJV.

I have concluded that the problems encountered in my life were not love issues, but rather flesh issues. Everyone connected to me through a relationship, friendship, fellowship and family is included in this misunderstanding. I now realize that lust provides for fleshly fulfillment, but has absolutely nothing to do with love. Love conquers the flesh; corrects lust and releases passion, stops pain, runs from hurt, shuns distraction, replaces abandonment, heals rejection, gives evil a run for its money and provides awesome conversation to relationships.

There is an Oracle of Love which exists and we all must access it if we want our love desires fulfilled. I am talking about God and the bedroom. We call it the master bedroom, I call it the love chamber - a place for the bride and groom, where history writes the ceremonial love story of two. In this place, spiritual elevation and word meditation become one, resulting in divine manifestation.

To attain this place, one must die in order to become one with God. This is called the love chamber.

Allow me to take you on a journey through the love chamber, its life cycle and mystery story. Paul talks about this in the Bible in Ephesians 5:32. *"This is a great mystery, that I speak concerning Christ and the church. This is intercession, yes intercession, we often associate this word with prayer and communing with God"*. This is correct, however it doesn't end there – things have only   just begun. That is why this book is called love, the unfinished chapter.

We know the dictionary's definition of love and we've also heard others express their opinions on love. There are seminars on love; the topic of love has been a great discussion piece and even television offers its version of love in an attempt to control the masses' view of love from their perspective and devilish standpoint. Religion provides the biblical point of view through preaching, teaching, serving and the list goes on and on.

 Love is not just a definition; it is not a storybook nor movie. Love isn't confined to a relationship between boyfriend and girlfriend, nor is it limited to the institution of marriage. While these are excellent within themselves, they are not the end. The Bible says in John 3:16 – *"God so loved the world that He gave His only begotten son that whosoever believeth in Him should not perish, but have everlasting life"*.

This means we are going to live an everlasting life through the promise of Love which God has shown unto us. Love never dies; it is eternal. The Bible says in Revelation 1:8 – *"I am Alpha and Omega; the beginning and the ending, says the Lord, which is, and which was, and which is to come, the Almighty".*

There are several points I am trying to make from this chapter as they relate to my life:

- We all have love inside of us
- There will always be a vacuum until it is acknowledged
- Things we pursue in the name of love are desires of the flesh
- We need to connect to the oracle of love
- Our love with Him will be made perfect when we depart from our flesh in death

We All Have Love Inside Us

You may be asking, "If we have love inside, then why do we keep searching for love?" The answer to this question rests in the notion that what lies on the inside, must be activated and realized. So far we have learned that God is love and His Spirit is in us. Mankind is a three-dimensional being. There is a Body, a Soul and a Spirit. The body is made of clay which serves as a vessel to carry the spirit and the soul. The soul represents who we are, while the Spirit is God's presence inside of us; His breath which He placed within us to give life.

When we die, the spirit returns to God; the soul faces judgment and goes to either heaven or hell, while the flesh is buried in the ground to mix with mother earth from where it originated. Excellent right? The spirit in us is God. He gave part of himself to us so that we may live. The spirit of God is that still quiet voice that will always tell us not to commit evil, which we refer to as 'The Conscience'. The spirit of God convicts us when we do wrong and causes us to experience feelings of remorse, whereby we ask for forgiveness from God.

If God is Love and His spirit is in us, don't you see that love dwells within us? The reason it takes so much time for us to realize this is mentioned in Galatians 5:16-17, "*This I say, walk in the Spirit, and you will not fulfill the lust of the flesh. For the flesh lusteth against the Spirit and the Spirit against the flesh: and these are contrary the one to the other: so that ye cannot do the things that ye would.*"

Flesh will always desire to be fulfilled and will always act contrary to what the spirit of God wants. This is why we are constantly divided in the choices and decisions we make. Jesus told His disciples in Mathew 26:41, "*Watch and pray, that ye enter not into temptation: the spirit is indeed willing, but the flesh is weak.*" This is a perfect example of how flesh wants to do the opposite of what God desires. God is love and His spirit in us will enable us to be carriers of His love.

The things you see and interpret as love are just mere imaginations influenced by the devil through your flesh to divert your attention from what is dormant within you.

Whenever you surrender to the desires of the flesh, you have basically decided to walk according to the way of the world. In 1John 2:16-17, he says "*For all that is in the world, the lust of the flesh, and the lust of the eyes, and the pride of life is not of the Father, but is of the world. And the world passeth away, and the lust thereof: but he that doeth the will of God abideth forever*" The spirit of God - which is His deposit of true love in every human, stays dormant when we obey the flesh or pursue love in the flesh.

There Will Always be a Vacuum Until it is Acknowledged

How can you be satisfied with the flesh? It is not possible. According to the Bible, the lust of the flesh and its fulfillment doesn't last. It comes and goes and leaves you more empty and unfulfilled. Until you recognize that true love is already deposited within you, you will always run from pillar to post looking for fulfillment.

There is no real joy or lasting satisfaction in pursuing the desires of the flesh. Since we are told in 1 John 2:17 that the world will pass away and the lusts thereof; how then can you obtain satisfaction from pursuing things of the flesh? You must acknowledge the spirit of God residing within you; then and only then will you begin to experience His love.

Instead of searching outside, look inwards today and start utilizing the love of God which is already available to you. One good thing about unveiling God's love, is that it touches every part of your body, soul and spirit.

It changes your destiny because when you lust, you deviate from God's plan for your life and walk astray. The minute you return to His plan for your life - you will begin to walk in the right direction, destiny and purpose, which will bring new meaning to your life.

Another point to note is that 'when that which is perfect' comes, it chases away the partial - which is the flesh. Love fills you, conquers flesh, heals you and corrects lust. Instead of pursuing things which have no joy, you will pursue everlasting life which can only be attained from God.

Things We Pursue in the Name of Love are Desires of the Flesh

Coming to the realization that God's love is already deposited within us, often proves to be difficult. From the time were born, we are socialized to associate love with gratifications of the flesh. The Bible tells us in 1John 2:16-17; *"For all that is in the world, the lust of the flesh, and the lust of the eyes, and the pride of life - is not of the Father, but is of the world."* When we chase these things, we are deceiving ourselves because they will never satisfy us.

According to Galatians 5:19, *"Now the works of the flesh are manifest, which are these; Adultery, fornication, uncleanness, lasciviousness, idolatry, witchcraft, hatred, variance, emulations, wrath, strife, seditions, heresies, envying, murders, drunkenness, reveling, and such like: of which I tell you before as I have also told you in time past, that they which do such things shall not inherit the kingdom of God"*

Pre-marital sex is fornication and those who engage shall not inherit the kingdom of God. A lot of relationships today are based purely on sex and ironically, many proclaim love in this kind of entanglement. How can you feel love when you are used by someone to satisfy their flesh? Sometimes you hear the term 'friends with benefits', which I believe is the highest form of violation. Until you realize that you are walking down the wrong path and return to your senses, your flesh will gradually lead you to hell.

We Need to Connect to an Oracle of Love

If you desire true love, you need to rise to the realm that takes you directly to the Oracle of Love. We know the oracle of love is God Himself and for you to attain His gift, you must enter into His Holy chamber: the unification between bride and groom which represents Christ and the Church.

To access the Oracle, you must meet the requirements. God demands nothing less than obedience, faith, righteousness and a clean heart. He hates sin and all appearances of evil. The Bible says in Hebrews 9:6, *"But without faith, it is impossible to please Him: for he that comes must first believe that He is a rewarder of them that diligently seek Him."*

It doesn't end with being obedient or righteous. You must diligently seek God to gain access to His chambers.

If you can enter this shrine, you will enter the everlasting love of God. There are steps to take now to start the process:

- You must be born again
- You must remain in Christ (2 Cor 5:17)
- You must diligently seek the oracle of love
- You must forsake the flesh and its desires

Surrendering your life to Christ is the first thing you should do to overcome the flesh. When you surrender your life to Christ, the spirit of God in you will be unleashed and the war against the flesh will become easy. After this, you must totally commit to the things of God and recognize His supremacy over all. When you get to this point - forsake the flesh and its demands.

When you are truly committed to God, He will unleash the power of His love upon you. Loneliness, hurt, betrayal, emptiness and depression will all disappear because of God's Supreme power working within you.

The love between God and man will be made perfect after we shed the carnal flesh in death, then we will meet Him. He made a promise in John 3:16, *"For God so loved the world that He gave His only begotten son; that whosoever believeth in Him shall not perish but have everlasting life"*

> ### *Our Love with Him will be Made Perfect When We Depart from our Flesh in Death.*

This is the perfection of God's love that even after death, we will live in His kingdom forever and ever.

At that time, there will be a marriage ceremony between the Lamb and His bride, which is the church of Jesus Christ. Those who merit attendance shall be there to witness the unification between Christ and His church. All you need to understand is that unless you are qualified to attend that wedding ceremony - Love will remain an unfinished chapter in your life. Keep nurturing love and building it until you get invited on that last day.

Chapter Nine

Love Found Me in Unchartered Territory

As I write this chapter, several major doors of my life are now open to an unknown audience who will draw their own perspective, viewpoint, and experience from what I share. Now, I want those reading this chapter to know how love found me in unchartered territory. What I am about to share is very important and is why I love this scripture: "*O taste and see that the Lord is good, blessed is the man that trusteth in Him*", Psalms 34:8. This verse sets the stage for the showdown of my life. Well, here I go…

Love found me in an unchartered territory for real. The definition of the word 'unchartered' is; 'not authorized or an area of land or sea not mapped or surveyed' - which means empty, void or not developed. I've had several failed relationships and friendships. Need I mention the 'sexcapades' encountered during the dark period of my life. I was unaware that a word even existed for my sexually-explicit acts until now. 'Sexcapade' means; sexual or illicit affair. Despite the power of this word, I don't believe it gives credence to my life. My life was full of freakish, immoral and crazy sexual appetites so intense, that the word 'sexcapade' lacks in meaning compared to the life I lived.

It was spring and the inception of an uncharted route; a life of sex, drugs, alcohol and more sex. I was raised within a very strict family with strong moral principles which I adhered to for a while - before I embarked upon an experimental journey of addiction and a quest for love. I was in the biggest fight of my life due to various temptations. You see, making money was easy; it came with private sexual encounters and more money, which meant taking my clothes off for whatever, whoever, whenever. This adventure went on and on and on.

Friends were a huge part of my life during this time; be careful whom you call friends. I say this because the people I called friends, were secretly planning my demise or might I say 'death sentence.' I don't know if they truly knew what they were getting me into, but they were always up to something regarding my life - after all, we were in a very competitive business. I met a very attractive female who appeared to have everything together - at least that's what I thought, but little did I know that she was a dangerous trap. You see God was talking to me while my friends were encouraging me to have sex with her. God was saying don't; they were saying "Man get that, man you need to go ahead and get that booty".

The pressure was on, in unchartered territory. I was out there now; bodies, money, sex, orgies - you name it, they were all available. I had the body, the smile, brown eyes and the desire to fulfill anyone's appetite - for a price of course. The word appetite is defined as a desire to satisfy a bodily need - especially food due to hunger. Appetites exist within all forms of life and regulate adequate energy intake to maintain metabolic needs. How do I link appetite to sex? Well, everyone needs food and knowing what kind of food you want makes it that much easier.

I became food to anyone willing to pay the price of enjoying what was prepared on my body.

Sex has a variety of appetites - you just need to know the person's favorite meal and feed them well. In my case, when I was high on drugs I could perform and do certain things with my body that others could not. In saying this, only my audience and associates could tell me what I was doing because I was unaware of my actions due to the drugs.

Let's go back to the day of the setup; the conversation with my friends. It appeared as if I was talking to them and God at the same time.

God was speaking to me saying "*Do not sleep with the young lady*"; all my friends were saying "Get that, get that" and I was saying "Why not, why not?". Ultimately, my friends and the desires of my flesh overpowered God's words. I now fully understand the word 'temp-taste-shun' (temptation). The word 'temp' is Satan; the word taste is me and the word 'shun' is God saying "*Shun the very appearance of sin*". I desired to sleep with the aids virus; Yes, she was HIV positive. Believe me, when I found out later - I was filled with pain and cold chills. Even while writing this chapter I experienced the very same feelings.

She died later from what appeared to be HIV- yet I am still here. Interestingly enough, before her death she requested to meet with me. Her family informed me she was asking about me and wanted to talk. During this particular time, I was in a committed relationship, so I decided not to open old wounds.

I now understand why God told me not to touch her; His love found me in unchartered territory for real. My God! My God! With tears in my eyes, He loved me even in this place and allowed me to escape destruction. You see, I created what I wanted love to be, but it only fulfilled an illusion and fantasy in my life.

God's design for our life is the place called paradise; heaven or eternity - the ultimate abode or place of the just. This is where life has already ordained our destiny while we try to create what He has already formed. In Jeremiah 1:5 – *"Before I formed thee in the belly I knew thee, and before thou camest forth out of the womb I sanctified thee, and I ordained thee a prophet unto the nation"*.

I was already set apart for love; I was ordained in love and made to love and to be loved by a nation - not unchartered things or the thoughts I created and called love. This only represented lust. Lust comes from the word luxury, which means 'something that is not essential, but provides pleasure and comfort'. It also means 'something which is considered an indulgence rather than a necessity'.

Below are a few things I want you to understand from my experience:

- Selling your body for sex is not worth the sacrifice
- Evil communication corrupts good manners
- Destiny can be delayed, but not denied
- God knows who we are
- His love finds us anywhere, anytime

Selling Your Body for Sex Isn't Worth the Sacrifice

Based on my experience, it's obvious that being a sex worker doesn't pay and isn't worth the sacrifice. Whether a prostitute or gigolo - they are one in the same. Believe me, the money you make will never be enough to pay for the consequences of these experiences.

Multiple dangers are involved with using your body as a tool for sale. You could possibly contract a disease or lose your sanity. In my case, I became addicted to drugs in order to help me function as a stallion. Drug addiction has destroyed and wrecked the lives of countless young men and women today. They indulge or experiment with drugs, while unaware of the fact they could ruin their lives, destitute and hopeless.

The Bible explicitly condemns the act of using our bodies for immorality. We are told that our bodies are the temple of the Holy Spirit and should be presented as a living sacrifice, holy and acceptable unto God. We don't possess the right to use our body in a corrupt manner because it is not ours.

Your life is in danger if you continue selling your body for sex and perverse acts. The Bible has warned, "*The soul that sinneth shall die*"; and this is no joke, I almost did.

Evil Communication Corrupts Good Manners

1 Corinthians 15:33, it states; "*Be not deceived; evil communication corrupts good manners*" There is a very popular, well-known proverb that says, "Show me your friends and I will tell you who you are."

Another wise saying is an African adage; "If a goat that doesn't eat yam starts to follow the one that eats yam, it will develop the appetite for yam". Both wise sayings teach the same principles. You must be careful when choosing friends or those in your surroundings. Making the wrong choice may cost you your life.

I had friends, but they were the wrong influences for my life. Instead of pulling me away from a dirty lifestyle, they were encouraging my lewd behavior. Take inventory regarding how your friends have affected your life, positively or negatively.

When you hang with prostitutes or gigolos, you will eventually join them and start justifying your decisions to support your life style. Prevent destruction and evaluate your relationships today. When I met the lady with HIV, my friends were encouraging me to have sex with her. If God had not been there in the unchartered territory, I often wonder what would have happened - death of course.

Destiny Can Be Delayed Not Denied

Destiny can be delayed but not denied. During this time, I was wallowing in sin and ignorance, not knowing that later I would become a prophet of God. I mean, look at me now. I am propagating the gospel on the greatest commandment - Love. If someone told me back then that I would find true love and teach others, my response would have been; "There is no such thing as true love." Thank God it later found me.

The devil uses confusion and lust in an attempt to delay our God-designed destinies. You may believe your life has no purpose now, until you encounter and experience love in that forbidden land. It requires an open heart and an alertness to answer the call of love in an unchartered territory. If it found me, I believe it will surely find you.

God is ready to use you today. He has already mapped out a course for your life. Instead of delaying it further, you can say no to the devil's devices by obeying the Bible which says, *"Submit yourselves therefore to God. Resist the devil, and he will flee from you"* James 4:7. If you can say no to lust today, the devil will flee from you and your destiny will begin to manifest.

God Knows Who We Are

I love the verse in the Bible where God said, "*Before I formed thee in the belly, I knew thee; and before thou camest forth out of the womb, I sanctified thee, and I ordained thee a prophet unto the nations*" Jeremiah 1:5. In my case, this scripture has been fulfilled and proved right. God formed me, watched over me in the belly, sanctified me and transformed me into a prophet.

He patiently watched over me and gave me enough time to come to my senses. When danger and death appeared in an unchartered territory, He stretched forth His hands, blocked it and delivered me. Today I am living according to His will. What am I saying? God knows each and every one of us; He made us in His own image and after His own likeness.

He is forever ready to intervene in our lives when faced with dangerous situations, until we realize how important God's love is for our life and our destiny.

It is important to understand that we were destined to be here for God's purpose. Each of us came from God with a glorious destiny. He knows us by name and our destinies are in His hands. No matter where we see ourselves now or in the future, we must remember that God knows who we are and what He has placed within us.

His Love Can Find You Anywhere and Anytime

If God is Omnipresent, it means He is everywhere. If His spirit is living inside of us, that means He sees us wherever we are. If you believe this, you should understand that God's love can find you anywhere and anytime.

I was told a story about a man who didn't believe God existed. One day, his baby became sick and was rushed to the hospital. At the head of his sick bed, the father placed a sign which read 'God is nowhere.' When he left the boy alone for a few seconds and returned, he saw that the sign was changed to 'God is now here.'

He changed it back to the original wording, yet it happened three more times. He decided to hide to see who was separating the words. When he hid and watched, he saw his baby - who was unable to talk or walk, crawl up to the sign and separate the words 'nowhere' to 'now here.' The man was shocked - yet moved in his heart and as a result, he repented and gave his life to God. Never doubt that even in that unchartered territory, God's love can still find you.

Chapter Ten

You can't schedule love

Who knows the definition of love? The definition we know comes from man. In other words, what we know and understand about love is based upon man's theory of love. This theory is based upon a faulty concept and foundation which have saturated our life since its inception. Thus, our experience with love is flawed. We have accepted it in our minds, put it into our hearts, expressed it with our mouth, gave it to friends, family, business partners and churches. We've rented it to our relationships and loaned it to our marriages.

Love is not a refrigerator; it exudes heat and warmth. Love is similar to a summer breeze during the winter cold. We hear people say time waits for no one; well it does, it waits for everyone. It won't allow you to stop it from moving into the love moment.

Love is never wrong, however attitudes toward love may be wrong. Placing love in the life of someone with the wrong motive or misguided concept of love, causes pain. There is no such thing as unconditional love. Love is benevolent and spends a lifetime taking care of its family. If we could only understand the power of family and love, then we would discover there is an inheritance we receive from God when we love. Oh yes! When love and life come together, the universe balances its eternal power and introduces a rhythm unknown to our cognitive reasoning.

You see love is projected, then expressed; when love is projected, it extends above and beyond boundaries. When love goes out, it always returns home safely. Love's only assignment is to give and not to take. Love is perfect and anything which is perfect doesn't require enhancement. 1 Corinthians 13:10 says; *"But when that which is perfect come, then that which is imperfect shall be done away"*.

There are multiple ways to define and describe the concept of love. From the Author's point of view, no human can schedule love. Time waits for no one, but believe me when I tell you, Love waits for everyone.

Let's explore some descriptions of love from various sources which will allow us to further understand love from several characteristics:

- What is love?
- Characteristics of love
- The difference between love and time
- Perfection in love

What is Love?

The simplest definition of love which cannot be disputed is found in the book of 1 John 4:8 - *"He that loveth not knoweth not God; for God is love."* If God is love, that means 'Love is God,' So whenever you want to understand love, think about God and if you want to know who God is - think of love. Mark 12:28-30 admonishes us to first love God, then love ourselves and our neighbors. He takes it further in the book of Matthew 5:43-48 were he tells us to love our enemies.

Love is a lifestyle and not just a warm, fuzzy feeling. In Luke 6: 30-36, Jesus further explained what love should look like among Christians. He says: "*Give to every man that asketh of thee; and of him that taketh away thy goods ask them not again. And as ye would that men should do to you do ye also to them likewise. For if ye love them which love you, what thank have ye? For sinners also love those that love them. And if ye do good to them which do good to you, what thank have ye? For sinners also do even the same. And if ye lend to them of whom ye hope to receive back, what thank have ye? For sinners also lend to sinners to receive as much again. But love ye your enemies, and do good, and lend, hoping for nothing again; and your reward will be great, and ye shall be the children of the Highest. For He is kind unto the unthankful and to the evil. Be ye therefore merciful as your father also is merciful.*"

Other definitions of love are from those who define love based on the feelings associated with love.

- According to Paulo Coelho in his book *Novel of Obsession*; "Love is an untamed force. When we try to control it, it destroys us. When we try to imprison it, it enslaves us. When we try to understand it, it leaves us feeling lost and confused."
- According to Honore de Balzac; "The more one judges, the less one loves."
- According to Louis de Bernieres in *Corelli's Mandoline*: "Love is a temporary madness, it erupts like volcanoes and then subsides. And when it subsides, you have to make a decision. You have to work out whether your roots have been so entwined together that it is inconceivable that you should ever part. Because this is what love is: Love is not breathlessness, it is not excitement, it is not the promulgation of promises of

eternal passion, it is not the desire to mate every second minute of the day, and it is not lying awake at night imagining that he is kissing every cranny of your body? No, don't blush, I am telling you some truths. That is just being 'in love,' which any fool can do. Love itself is what is left over when being in love has burned away, and this is both an art and a fortunate accident."

- According to Katharine Hepburn in *Me: Stories of my Life* – "Love has nothing to do with what you are expecting to get - only with what you are expecting to give - which is everything."

These quotes were formed from the writers' opinions and experiences. When you open your heart to true love, you may develop an agreement of words to best define what you feel. Therefore, one undeniable truth is that true love can only be understood through God in order for it to be complete and fruitful.

Characteristics of Love

Love has many characteristics which the Bible enumerated in 1 Corinthians 13:4-8 as follows:

- Love is patient. If you love someone, you can bear their faults and whatsoever delay they may put you through.
- Love is kind. Extending goodwill and generosity to others shows that you love them.
- It does not envy. Instead of hating someone when good things happen to them, you are happy and rejoice with them.

- It does not boast. Showing off or talking about what you are or who you are to make others unhappy is not found in love
- It is not proud. Esteeming yourself higher than others is not found in love.
- It does not dishonor others. When you love someone, you protect their dignity.
- It is not self-seeking. Looking for your personal satisfaction first before others is not love.
- It is not easily angered. Little things make you angry with someone doesn't show love at all.
- It keeps no record of wrongs. You remember all the wrongs someone did to you even if many years has passed is not love. Love forgives and forgets.
- Love does not delight in evil but rejoices with the truth. Lying against others or supporting evil is not love. It hates oppression.
- It always protects. Love covers others from harm both physically and emotionally.
- It always trusts. Love believes in someone's sincerity, words and action totally
- It always hopes. Love believes that what it wants to happen will always come to pass.
- It always perseveres. It persists in the face of disappointments and difficulties until it achieves what it planned
- Love never fails. It will always answer whenever it is called. It doesn't disappoint.
- Love is eternal. It lasts forever.

Wow! I counted sixteen characteristics of love which encompass our needs. I can add my own as 'Love is complete.' Can't you see the completeness of love? If you have true love, you can achieve everything. True love comes with sixteen responsibilities we are expected to fulfill towards our loved ones. So, the next time you want to say those powerful three words, think twice and be sure you truly mean what you say.

The Difference Between Love and Time

'Time waits for no man' and 'Love waits for all men'. Time and love are extremely important things which should be taken seriously. God controls both. The way you handle time and love determines your life. Losing either of the two will lead regret.

Time…...

In Ecclesiastics 3:1-8, the Bible says:

To everything there is a season and a time to every purpose under the heaven:

A time to be born, and a time to die; a time to plant, and a time to pluck up that which is planted;

A time to kill, and a time to heal; a time to break down, and a time to build up;

A time to weep, and a time to laugh; a time to mourn, and a time to dance;

A time to cast away stones, and a time to gather stones together; a time to embrace, and a time to refrain from embracing;

A time to get, and a time to lose; a time to keep, and a time to cast away;

A time to rend, and a time to sew; a time to keep silence, and a time to speak;

A time to love, and a time to hate; a time of war, and a time of peace.

Solomon, one of the wisest men in the Bible took time to understand the concept of time and passed it on to us without mincing words. There is a time for everything under the sun. A time to love and a time to hate. This means that no matter what you are going through, it will surely pass and when it does, it cannot be recalled.

'Today is the tomorrow we waited for yesterday'; Time moves and never returns. Time also projects the occurrences of events. We can even pay for time.

Love.....

Love, on the other hand cannot be planned, projected, scheduled or bought. Love cannot be predicted because sometimes, the people you love may be so undeserving that you question why you are wasting time on them. The prioritized people in our life is our family. I believe if we were given the option to choose our parents and siblings, most would never choose the family they actually grew up with. You may not understand this point if you were blessed with a great family.

Many are currently experiencing hell because of parents, siblings, children and spouses. Ironically, it doesn't matter how bad they are - you love them despite the negative actions and words and there is this sense of hope that one day things will be alright. You can only be hopeful in such a situation because of love.

Love begins at birth. Your first experience with love comes through the actions of your parents and through their demonstration of love, you love them in return. As time progresses, you extend love to your entire family. Suffice it to say, with this comes a feeling of possession; "These people are mine and I must protect them." Why do you think children fight when someone speaks ill of their family? It is an outward display of their love and their need to protect their family, even though they are not mature enough to understand.

Perfection in Love

You may not be able to schedule love, but love makes everything perfect when it arrives. There is no doubt about this; God is love and He being perfect, tells us to be perfect like Him. Matthew 5:48. When God takes control of your life, even the crooked ways are made straight. Isaiah 45:2. This is how love works as well.

When you are with those who truly love you, they will help bring out the best in you. They build you up in areas where you are lacking and in doing so, perfection is eventually achieved. If your friends, spouse or family always try to expose your inadequacies, they do not love you.

Love makes you feel perfect and whole. Open your heart today, as it will come to you unexpectedly. You can't schedule love, but it will last forever.

Chapter Eleven

Love Has No Divorce

It was fall of the mid-nineties and unknowingly, I entered into the scariest union of my life. I became connected to someone I did not know - neither did I understand the person's past or present life. What I had to face was the darkest side of the 'other me'. Yes, that's right - the other me. After all, the bible says "the two become one Hell – Oh, I mean one flesh". I gave it my all thinking it was the right thing to do. I sincerely thank God for not saying "one spirit".

Well, if I had known the unknown - I would have skipped this assignment which caused me to question God. What happened? What went wrong? What did I do? How did I get here? And the statement Adam made - you know, the blame game. Yes - the blame game. "The woman you gave me made me do it" - Do what? Alter our destiny; but only when I ate the forbidden fruit, death was introduced and I was naked and alone.

At this particular point in my life, everything that was eternal became external. I was in a clash with - or should I say 'in a showdown with' an eternal God and the external evil in battle with this union. Needless to say, I took my eyes off God and myself and loved her more than God. It cost me everything - my destiny, time and a lot of pain. You can never save the bride until you have saved the groom. The Bible says we can do all things through Christ which strengthen us.

You cannot love a woman or man more than you love God. We must love God more than anything; it's called a love affair with the king and not of things. I loved her with everything that was in me and tried expressing it every way possible but she did not love herself. The wounds of childhood pain, issues and circumstances caused her to close her heart to love – therefore, as much as I loved her she was not able to embrace or receive it. In essence, I was forcing on her what she did not have to give.

If only I continued to love God and Him alone. It would have required her to love my God and God would have shown her how to love me. Instead, my relationship became a God to me and I stopped following the God of the universe and His plans for our destiny. Believe me, this was one of the greatest regrets of my life. Thank God I came to my senses before too late.

If you have not walked in my shoes, the devil may still tempt you to divorce the love of your life, question God and seek things which ultimately result in you leaving the King. I sincerely wish that after reading this chapter, you are in the right position to prevent this from happening.

The lessons and conclusions of this experience are:

- We make wrong choices sometimes
- Wrong choices can alter our destiny
- Relationships based on the wrong foundation will surely crash
- Don't remove your eyes from God
- Don't let anything come between you and God
- If you remain faithful to God, those around you will follow suit

We Make Wrong Choices Sometimes

Everyone is prone to mistakes - therefore we make the wrong decisions sometimes. The sooner we realize this depend on God's guidance for every situation – our lives will become better. King Solomon had knowledge of this and made it clear in the Bible in Proverbs 3:5-6, "*Trust in the Lord with all your heart and lean not to your own understanding. In all your ways acknowledge him, and He will direct your path*".

If we learn to depend on God for guidance in our decisions, we will avoid pitfalls and terrible situations caused by our actions. The bible says we should trust in the Lord with all our hearts; meaning, we must believe that He knows what is best for us. Had I trusted Him to direct me in my relationship, He would have made the perfect choice for my life - but instead, I relied on my own limited vision and got it wrong.

God is the only one who can see the end from the beginning. It is a mistake for us to believe we can predict the outcome of an event based on our own understanding. We can never be right depending on our understanding.

We are told to acknowledge Him in all our ways – not "*in some ways*," Solomon said "In all your ways"- meaning both big and small things, we should make God the center everything.

Do not think there is anything too small for God. He is concerned about the smallest, minute details of your life. If you acknowledge Him in all things, then you totally trust Him.

Finally, the Bible tells us that when we seek God, He will direct our path. Let us always seek God's opinion and direction first, because He sees the end from the beginning.

Wrong Choices Alter our Destiny

Wrong actions alter destinies. This occurs when we depend on our own limited understanding to carry out actions contrary to the will of God for our lives. Only God knows the course of our lives because it is His design. When we leave Him and do what we want, our destinies are destroyed.

Becoming entangled with people who are not aligned with the vision of our lives, also destroys our destinies. I got carried away by mischief and landed inside a deep pit that required God's intervention to save me. I made the wrong choice and it nearly cost my relationship with God.

I made a selfish choice that diverted my attention away from God. I lost focus of what was important and sacred to me. This caused me to pursue things I lusted. If you ignore the source of your light - darkness will cover you and the presence of darkness brings death. No matter what you do today, never choose anything to jeopardize your relationship with God.

Relationships Based on the Wrong Foundation Will Crash

The only sure foundation which stands is built on God. This is why the Bible tells us in 2 Timothy 2:19- *"Nevertheless, the foundation of the Lord standeth sure, having this seal, the Lord knoweth them that are His and everyone who calls on the name of the Lord must depart from iniquity"* You cannot build a relationship on love without the approval of God Almighty. When He is at the center of that union - rain and storms may come, but the relationship will stand unshaken.

My relationship crashed because it was created on the foundation of sin. We were so full of ourselves that we neglected the Lord Almighty - the oracle of love we needed. I almost died before realizing the relationship wasn't built on the right foundation. I mean, how could I love a woman more than God? I traded my love for the King with my love for things.

Thank God it was only a fusion of the flesh and not a fusion of the spirit. My relationship crashed because my partner and I did not allow room for God's dwelling. She struggled with pain and sad memories of her past and her heart wasn't ready to love nor accept love. Thank God for the power which we receive from Christ. I came to my senses and decided that my love for God supersedes another. Although my relationship crashed, I was saved.

When You Remove Your Eyes from God, You crash

When you turn your eyes away from God, you will crash. This is also true in reverse; when God removes Himself from you, you will surely crash as well. Ultimately, we need God in order to survive. In 2 Samuel 22:3, *"And David spoke unto the Lord the words of this song in the day that the Lord had delivered him out of the hand of all his enemies, and out of the hand of Saul: And he said, The Lord is my rock, and my fortress, and my deliverer; The God of my rock; in him will I trust: he is my shield, and the horn of my salvation, my high tower, and my refuge, my savior; thou savest me from violence"*

King David recognized that if we did not keep our eyes entirely on God, we would make mistakes leading to our downfall. The only hope we have is that God loves to the point where even when we sin - He still waits for us to realize our mistakes and return to Him. I was blessed to return unto God. He in turn, forgave me and picked me up from the ground. This specific experience is something I would not even wish on my enemies.

Do not forget this verse of the Bible; James 4:8, "*Draw near to God, and He will draw near to you. Cleanse your hands, you sinners; and purify your hearts, you double-minded*" If you focus on God, He will focus on you. There is no divorce from God. He simply loves us forever.

Don't Allow Anything to come Between You and God

Why do you think couples who exchange marital vows suddenly separate? I mean, they vowed to love each other 'til death do we part'- what happened along the way? Why have they become enemies unable to bear the sight of each other? The answer is simple; they allowed things to come between them. It could be minor issues or a matter which could've been settled amicably - yet because of ignorance or a lack of God's presence, the devil blew things out of proportion.

In our relationship with God, we shouldn't allow things to come between us and the love of God. The Bible asked this question in Romans 8:35-39, "*What shall separate us from the love of Christ? Shall tribulation, or distress, or persecution, or famine, or nakedness, or peril, or sword? As it is written, for thy sake we are killed all the day long; we are accounted as sheep for the slaughter*".

"*Nay, in all these things we are more than conquerors through Him that loved us.*

For I am persuaded, that neither death, nor life, nor angels, nor principalities, nor powers, nor things present, nor things to come,

Nor height, nor depth, nor any other creature, shall be able to separate us from the love of God, which is in Christ Jesus our Lord."

If you allow yourself to become separated from God's love, you've lost touch with God. Is it not better to forsake all these things and hold unto the Lord? The Bible says in Mark 8:36, *"For what shall it profit a man, if he shall gain the whole world, and lose his own soul?"* Never allow anything to occupy you more than God because with His Love, there is no divorce.

If You Remain Faithful to God, Those Around You Will Follow

A man of God was once asked if he was faithful to his wife. Do you know what he said? He stated; "I am faithful to God and my wife is benefitting from that faithfulness." Wonderful, right? In other words, if we remain faithful to God - those around us are affected and will remain faithful to Him as well. Had I continue to love God, my partner would have joined me and allowed God to teach her the way of love.

The truth is that sometimes we allow the devil to lure us away. This is why the Bible says, *"Evil communication corrupts good manners"* It takes a determined spirit to remain unshaken when faced with temptation. Resist the devil, stand your ground and defend your love for God.

Chapter Twelve

Love; The Master Piece

I would like to declare that love always resumes where a painful memory ends. I see love so differently now because I walked away from what was too cheap for my priceless future. See, my love never ended - the events or story of my life ended. Then and only then did love appear right at the point where I thought it left me.

Love truly never ends; it begins where it stopped in you. Thus, I have concluded that love never competes with the lie you believe; the story you tell, the definition you create, those who violated or the pleasure resulting from the experience. Love waits and returns at the right moment.

I realize that I wasn't violated; I violated love, yet it allowed me to wait for its return. Love wasn't going to pay for the cheap lie holding on to the sinful nature within me, knowing there was a moral God waiting. This is why Revelation 1:8 says, "*I am alpha and omega; the beginning and the ending says the Lord, which is, and which was, and which is to come the Almighty.*"

Wow! Love is the Almighty - not my personal body; God just waited for my body to follow His perfect will. This can only happen when I meet him in the perfect place of truth.

The following will assist you personally in finding the perfect place of true love where God dwells:

- Love picks up where painful memories end
- You must walk away from the wrong path
- Love leaves when it is violated
- Love will always return
- Love never ends

Love Picks Up Where Painful Memories End

There are many people burdened by the betrayal of those who were supposed to love them. I believe everyone has a story of betrayal, disappointment, hurt, abandonment, etc. We all have healed wounds and some that are in the process of being healed. What is interesting is that in order for hurt to be painful - it must come from the people we truly loved. Some people dwell on issues for so long time, their relationships are unknowingly affected. They often don't intend to hurt others, but the unresolved issues cause them to push people away, hence the circle continues.

Betrayal is part of our existence. The Bible says in Jeremiah 17: 9-10, *"The heart is deceitful above all things; and desperately wicked: who can know it? I the Lord search the heart, I try the reins, even to give every man according to his ways, and according to the fruits of his doings..."* If God is the only one who can understand the heart of man, how can you avoid being hurt by the people who pretend to love you?

Unfortunately, if you don't move on from painful memories, you will never experience love. When you are hurt, learn the lesson and move forward. Love is around the corner waiting to see if you drop that baggage of anger, vengeance, disappointment or pessimism before it enters. True love is forever ready to pick up the fragments of your shattered heart and piece them back together – but only if it is welcomed.

Here is what you can do to relieve your pain:

- Sit down and take an inward look at your life
- Try to understand what went wrong or what you did wrong
- If it is your fault, take note and avoid it in the future
- Forgive the person who hurt you
- Remember that your joy is from the Lord - not man
- Clear your heart of vengeful thoughts
- Ask God to send His true love your way so that you can heal.

Our problem is that we spend more time complaining when we are hurt, versus forgiving and forgetting. No one said it would be easy, but if you don't make a conscious effort to bounce back - how can love arrive and heal you? Love is waiting to enter immediately; you just have to clear your head of painful memories and give it a chance. You will thank me later.

You Must Walk Away from the Wrong Path

We know that love is the Master Piece right? We also know true love picks up where painful memories end - however, it is not for everyone. Unless you open your heart, it will not come. How can you open up to true love, you might ask? Walk away from the wrong path and stop playing with sin. Drop those acts which push God away from you and begin seeking

His face today or you will miss your opportunity for everlasting love.

If God is love and He hates sin, how will love come to a sinner? We see that true love is sacrificial as God demonstrated in John 3:16; we also learned that the more we show love to people - the more we receive. How then can someone whose heart is desperately wicked, understand and practice the demands of true love? You must change from bad to good; from darkness to light and from death to life.

There is no place for darkness in your life. If you are searching for true love and you find it difficult to forgive, then you haven't fully embraced love. Saying you love, yet you harbor unforgiveness is preposterous! What about the vengeful tendencies in you which people hate? How can you harbor such dirtiness and expect something perfect to come? You need to clean up your dirty floor before it can be spread with a white sheet.

The more you pursue sexual perversion - the more true love will elude you. Any relationship built on sin will always collapse and end in disappointment and betrayal. We all need to be loved, but we also need to love others.

For us to do so comfortably, we must define what's more important to us. True love or lust. The two cannot be combined. Choose one of the two because they can't exist side by side. If you pursue lust, true love will elude you; and if you pursue true love, lust will run away - but you will have your peace of mind.

Now you must make a decision and decide which way you are going to follow because there is absolutely no short cut to

God's love. You must be ready to give it all you have. Why not? There is no betrayal at all.

Love Leaves When Violated

You may be wondering how can one violate love and make it leave. Well, we have all done it, either knowingly or unknowingly. Since we are talking about true love, I'll start with the Master Himself. There are multiple ways we have violated the love of God. God told the people of Israel in Exodus chapter 20:2-5, "_I am the Lord your God, who brought you out of the land of Egypt, out of the house of bondage. You shall have no other gods before me. You shall not make for yourself a graven image or any likeness of anything that is in heaven above, or that is in the earth beneath, or that is in the water under the earth; you shall not bow down to them or serve them_" Also in Matthew 22:37, Jesus commanded, "_You shall love the Lord your God with all your heart, and with all your soul, and with all your mind._"

In the first commandment by God, the Israelites were told not to worship another God but to love only God who saved them.

As Christians, we believe in one God and worship Him, yet we are violating His commandment by having things in our lives which we love more than God. For example; power, popularity, money, material goods, prestige, vanity, pleasure, etc. The manner in which we pursue these things far exceed our pursuit of God. We only spare a few minutes of our time pursuing God - yet we give hours to things which have replaced God. Hence, the modern man of today is violating God's love by worshipping things outside of Him.

The second commandment was for us to love God with all our heart, soul and minds. Today Christians who profess love for God are in violation through the following:

- **Being Lukewarm**; God doesn't like lukewarm Christians. They hesitate in loving God and their fellow man. They know the truth, but find it hard to respond. They've experienced God's goodness and love from mankind, but close their hearts.
- **Indifference;** these are those people who adamantly refuse to think about love.
- **Ingratitude;** those who don't know the importance of thanksgiving for what God does for them.
- **Hatred for God**; seeing God as wicked for forbidding sin, judgment and harsh punishment

These are some of the ways in which we violate God's love. This also affects our relationship with others because if you don't know how to love God - how can you love your neighbor as required?

Love Will Always Return

The truth is that love will always find you again, no matter how long it takes. Jesus said in Revelation 3:20, "*Behold, I stand at the door, and knock: if any man hear my voice, and open the door, I will come into him and will sup with him, and he with me.*" This clearly shows that God is ready to love you any day or anytime, once you open yourself to Him. He is waiting, watching and even knocking. If you just open the door of your heart, He will enter and heal all your wounds and make things beautiful for you.

Love leaves when you violate it and returns when you call. Remember this; the next time your spirit is down because of betrayal, know that it's not the end of the road. Things will turn around once your heart is opened to God. Betrayals will end, relationships may end and friends may desert you - but your love will abide. When people leave your life, it may hurt; but hold firm to the fact that love always returns.

Love Never Ends

The Bible makes it clear in 1 Corinthians 13:8-10, "*Love never faileth: but whether there be prophecies, they shall fail; whether there be tongues they will cease; whether there be knowledge, it shall vanish away. For we know in part and we prophesy in part. But when that which is perfect is come, then that which is in part will be done away with*".

From this chapter, we understand that tongues shall cease, and knowledge will be brought to nothing. Love is the only perfect thing that chase the partial away.

God is everlasting and perfect. His love remains forever and ever. If He promises us an everlasting love, what possible excuse do we have for not loving Him with our entire being? Jesus commands His disciples in John chapter 13:34-35, "*A new commandment I give unto you, that you love one another; as I have loved you, that you also love one another. By this shall all men know that you are my disciples if you have love one to another*"

The only way to show the world that we are disciples of Christ is by loving one another. He commanded this to emphasize the importance of Love in God's kingdom. Even though you may be in a rough place right now, never give up on your search for true love. If you're wondering why your life is devoid of love, remember that the root of true love is God. Unless you receive it through Him, it is counterfeit love.

Love never ends. It abides forever and never fails. We mistakenly get into trouble by searching in the wrong places.

Conclusion......

To love and be loved is the greatest gift we can receive. Everyone wants true love and the only source thereof is from the oracle of love, which is God.

Because of heartbreak and betrayal, many choose a path which doesn't lead to true love.

While you may be in a state of confusion right now, there is still time to open your heart to the love you desire. Just remember that He is the only one able to provide what you want.

The first thing to do is to give your life to Christ and ask for His love. When He pours Himself into you, true love will be given.

Dedication.......

I want to honor my Abba Father who has given me the wisdom, fortitude, and strength to embark upon this journey; without Him none of this would have been possible. It is through His love that I was able to complete this book and for that I'm grateful.

I dedicate this book to my oldest sister Regina Matthews, who passed away at an extremely pivotal time in my life. You were not only my sister, but a mentor and confidant. Thank you for the wisdom, love and support you deposited into my life. I certainly wish you were here to share this moment with me. To my mom and dad who raised eighteen children; thank you for carrying destiny and to my children for watching history unfold. To my other siblings, you have watched me grow and supported me in all my endeavors. To Bishop Rance and Mother Ellen Allen, thank you for your support and leadership during one of the most difficult periods in my life. Finally, to my administrator Retha Bryant and my entire ministry team; thank you for your unrelenting support, encouragement and prayers during the writing of this book.

About the Author.........

Prophet Laron Matthews is known as a seasoned man of God with character, integrity, wisdom, and great revelation of God's Word with Prophetic accuracy. He is a gifted communicator to all facets of people linking the young and old together to accomplish the vision of Christ, (John 17:22) with passion and love for the 21st century church (Proverbs 17:27). Through this vision he has crossed denominational barriers to bring the power of fellowship, friendship, and relationship with God's best interest at heart. *"A man that hath friends must shew himself friendly"* (Proverbs 18:24).

Prophet Matthews was born October 31, 1967 the seventh child of 18 children born to Bishop Nathaniel and Mrs. Suzanne Matthews. Prophet Matthews is a devoted parent and grandfather. He matriculated through Joliet Township High School Central, Joliet Junior College, The Economic Business Institute, Spencer College, and The Research Institute of America.

Prophet Matthews gave his life to Christ in October, 1994 and was licensed a Minister in February, 1996; appointed Chairman of the Finance Committee under the leadership of his father Bishop Nathaniel Matthews of *The Way of Life Holiness Church Inc.,* many other responsibility came from this gifted area. In July, 1997 he was ordained and appointed International Youth President of *Apostolic Assembly Way of Holiness Church of God Inc.,* under the Late Bishop George King. He was appointed Financial Accountability person for the Youth Department International and Chairman of the Youth Convention.

Prophet Matthews completed Ministerial Protocol and Etiquette for Leadership, Altar Workers Training, and received Apostolic Prophetic impartation in the ascension Office of Prophet in February 2001 and in September 2006 he was ordain to the office of Pastorate. Now currently conducting Prophetic explosion crusade meetings and conferences nationally; he is a former member of the Spanish Center of Will County where he was Chairman of the Finance Committee and was elected Treasurer of the Board and former liaison for the city Councilman of District 5 of Joliet, Illinois.

Prophet Matthews established the inner city counselors and training program for the Joliet Park District which reestablished and unified one of the greatest inter-governmental agreements in Will County; he was also a member of the Will County Gang Task Force.

Prophet Matthews established the Metropolitan Counseling and Advisory Organization of Will County reaching youth of all cultural backgrounds to build and motivate a positive mentoring program; a former faithful member and lead Prophet of *Holy Spirit Ministries International* under the Leadership of Pastor James E. Latimore Sr.; Prophet Matthews is presently senior Pastor of *Restoration Foundation Prophetic International Ministries*, Lansing IL, *Restoration Family Worship Center*, Montgomery AL, *Restoration Covenant Ministries*, Los Angeles, CA.

Prophet Laron Matthews is a graduate of American Bible University with a Masters Degree in Christian Counseling Licensed through the New Covenant Christian Counselors Association.

Prophet Laron Matthews is currently the overseer of a dynamic anointed Prophetic Encounter conference line Monday Saturday. 5:00 a.m. central time 12:00 midnight and every Wednesday Noon Day Prayer. 218-548-3684 passcode: 435160# You can also join Prophet Laron Matthews on blog-talk radio live every Sunday morning at 7:00 a.m. central time. Call into blog-talk radio at 424-222-5276. You can watch also Prophet Laron Matthews weekly on his very on Television Broadcast "The Prophetic Oil" at Preach The Word Worldwide Network. www.ptwwntv.com

~Also I heard the voice of the Lord saying, Whom shall I send, and who will go for us? Then said I, Here am I; send me..... Isaiah 6:8~